THE
JOURNEY

A Roadmap for Self-healing After Narcissistic Abuse

Meredith Miller

ISBN 978-1979693387
ISBN 1979693382

Cover Design: Red Raven Book Design
Interior Design: Red Raven Book Design
Back Cover Photo: Greg Lightner
Printed in USA

Disclaimer and Terms of Use: Meredith is not a medical doctor or therapist. She does not diagnose or treat disease. She does not give medical advice nor make claims or promises of curing any illness or disease. Your reliance upon information and content obtained by you at or through this publication is solely at your own risk. This holistic work is about empowerment, balancing body-mind-spirit, and improving self-care while expanding self-awareness in order to thrive in your life. Thank you for taking responsibility for yourself.

www.InnerIntegration.com

Dedication

This book is dedicated to all those who have been abused, manipulated, violated and mistreated.

I hope this roadmap will help you find your way out and forward.

You are strong and brave.
You are not alone.

Contents

Prologue

I believe we all have the right and responsibility to feel empowered, worthy and free.

My story of self-healing after narcissistic abuse began the day I realized that I'd been programmed to accept the Legacy of Abuse passed down my lineage for who knows how many generations. Where did it start? It's hard to know.

The Legacy of Abuse gets passed on trans-generationally without question as something normal and acceptable. When it's modeled by parents, it teaches children that's what love is. Kids then grow up to accept more abuse from others as adults or worse yet they become abusers themselves. Eventually the problem becomes pandemic.

Abuse is deeply woven through society from the macro to the micro level. I believe *the* problem in our world is that many families, corporations, workplaces, governments, media, entertainment, and even spiritual and religious organizations are functioning according abusive values and promoting the normalization of this behavior.

The human species is destroying the planet and robbing the wellbeing from future generations. Senseless wars are perpetuated and promoted causing more trauma and devastation. Millions of people go hungry every day. There are nearly six times as many vacant foreclosed homes as there are homeless people in the streets in America.

None of this makes any sense when you're looking at it from a perspective of empathy. Empathy is precisely what is lacking in the fabric of society.

I know that we can do better and I think you might agree.

I believe that we can create a better world. I believe this is our birthright and responsibility to ourselves, to the planet and to future generations.

I believe the change starts when the individual stands up and declares, "It ends with me."

This is no small thing.

Something incredible happens when you take a stand. As each individual stands up and speaks up in your interpersonal relationships, families and communities, you give permission to others to do the same.

As we collectively stop enabling and condoning the abuse of one another and this planet, things change. As we opt out of the reality paradigm of abuse, we ostracize the abusers instead of celebrating and promoting them.

I believe you can help heal the world by taking responsibility for yourself, standing up for yourself, and opting out of the abuse dynamic. As you work on self-healing after abuse, you can stand confidently and in integrity with your true self, owning your reality, and turning away from any new invitations to suffer abuse.

As you free yourself from abuse, you can live the life of purpose that you dream of. You can create a new sense of meaning in your life and make your soul's contribution, creating ripple effects in the world around you.

Imagine the world we would live in when instead of suffering in the powerlessness and struggling in the worthlessness of abuse, we are each living as empowered beings driven by purpose and making a difference.

You matter. You can help create a new way of life for yourself and generations to come.

Big hug to you!
Meredith

Introduction

Abuse can take many forms. These include mental, emotional, financial, sexual, physical, and spiritual. Many kinds of abuse are invisible yet leave long-lasting scars on the victims and survivors.

These invisible forms of abuse are rarely talked about yet incredibly common.

There is currently a silent pandemic leaving millions of people feeling alone and confused, struggling to escape the self-doubt, fear and so many unanswered questions. Invisible abuse is rarely talked about because of how hard it is to pin-point, even by mental health professionals.

Fortunately, there is a growing wealth of information available, particularly around the term *narcissistic abuse*. After discovering the keywords and digging for answers, the next step is figuring out what to do about it now.

It's important to understand that leaving the abusive person and educating yourself about the abuse is not the same as healing. This discovery is the actually start of the journey of self-healing after narcissistic abuse.

Awareness is the first step to change. The next step is to take action.

What Is Narcissistic Abuse?

Narcissistic abuse has classic, identifiable patterns of behavioral dynamics that are nearly identical regardless of country, culture, language, age, race, gender or socio-economic status. After sharing stories, many people say, "It's like they all read the same book!"

There are two phases of the narcissistic abuse cycle: idealization and devaluation. This is also known as the sweet-mean cycle. These phases are not necessarily linear in order as they are most often used in a back and forth game of intermittent reinforcement. They build you up and break you down over and over again. This is the trademark of narcissistic abusers.

When you see someone doing the build you up then break you down game, that's a major sign you're dealing with a manipulative character and the sooner you turn away the better.

During the idealization moments, the narcissistic manipulator uses love-bombing, an intense but shallow showering of attention via words and/or actions to seduce (though not always sexually) the target. Idealization is used in order to make the target feel special. It's the flattering words, gifts, exciting whirlwind dates, frequent and intense contact, early promises of a future together, and in some cases intense and early sex. There are certain characters who skip most of the flattery and just go directly for an intense and edgy sexual connection in order to create a strong emotional bond. There are others who are not sexual at all and use the intellect as their primary weapon of choice. In non-romantic interpersonal relationships, the idealization looks mostly like superficial praising and gushing or gift-giving. Idealization is also used when manipulators sense that the target is slipping away before they're done with him or her.

In relationships where the manipulator is grooming someone for the long-con, the initial love-bombing phase will go on for much longer. In situations where the manipulator is just looking for a temporary source of supply, the love-bombing will end much quicker because they won't need to invest as much in the seduction knowing that they will discard the target sooner rather than later. Jackson MacKenzie explains this dynamic in *Psychopath Free*[1] and his theory is one hundred percent accurate in the stories people tell me.

The idealization, while it looks quite pleasant, is actually very dangerous because it can appear to be genuine when in fact it is only being used as a form of manipulation to reel in a prey.

This is exactly how people get sucked in.

The idealization eventually gives false hope to the person who stays with the abuser. This false hope sounds like, "I just want to go back to the good times before... happened." "I know s/he has a sweet side too." "I know s/he can change and be the person I saw glimpses of during the relationship." Abusive people know they have to use idealization intermittently with the devaluation in order for the trick to work. Most of us wouldn't hang around people who are just assholes all the time.

The devaluation is when the narcissistic manipulator makes the target feel unworthy. This can be with words or actions. It's the backhanded put-downs, the little subtle digs here and there, the direct and explicit making fun of, the blatant criticism and cruelty. It's also the Silent Treatment after the target sets a boundary, calls out the abuser or doesn't give them what they wanted. It's the suddenly too busy for you attitude. It's using triangulation with another person i.e. someone the manipulator is attracted to, or someone who is amazing at doing what you do, someone who is like you in some way, or someone that means more to them or they spend more time with than you in order to incite jealousy, insecurity and the belief that you will never measure up. Triangulation can also be done with work, hobbies and even the use of substances.

The devaluation is a lot more obviously hurtful than the idealization, but even so it can be easy to miss the subtle, covert and unspoken forms of it until the target is in deep due to the slow progression over time.

A narcissistic character is looking for narcissistic supply. They are addicted to this form of energetic and emotional currency and they will do whatever it takes to get it. They desire and provoke both positive and negative supply from targets by systematically using intermittent idealization and devaluation. When manipulators are using idealization, they're looking for positive supply in the form of attention, adoration, devotion, sex, money, etc. When they are using devaluation, they're looking for negative supply in the form of anger, outrage, jealousy, emotional outbursts, fear, pain, etc.

In the case of an alcoholic, the addiction comes in a bottle and the abuse usually looks a lot more obvious like yelling and rage.

In the case of a narcissistic character,
both the abuse and the addiction are invisible.

This makes it even more confusing for the target to put his/her finger on exactly what is wrong. It's therefore very difficult to point out and explain to others.

This leaves the target feeling even more alone and confused in the
struggle.

This kind of abuse is silently happening on interpersonal, familial and societal levels. I believe it is the leading cause of loneliness, anxiety and depression in the world nowadays. If only depression carried a birth certificate, we might understand where it came from.

Narcissistic abuse has been going on for a long time, from the macro to the micro level in society, and it appears to be growing at exponential rates. Nowadays it's being normalized by the media and entertainment industries and promoted by many corporations and institutions.

The media often downplays narcissism as selfies and social media attention-seeking, when this is a very superficial and minimized portrayal of the amount of devastation that a narcissistic character can cause in the lives of others.

The entertainment industry tends to condone and celebrate narcissistic characters on screen, often making them likable and instilling the false hope that they will one day wake up and change, when that is most often just a fairy tale. Behind the scenes, the predatory and abusive behavior of many producers, directors, actors and media personalities is finally being exposed.

In the recent years we have also seen numerous abusive scandals coming to light in academic, religious and spiritual institutions. The common pattern of dealing with it tends to be immediately covering up this behavior and protecting the abusers instead of calling them out, often shaming and blaming the victims in the process. This is absolutely unacceptable.

We are living in a world run by the narcissistic and sociopathic values of many corporations, governments, schools, religious and spiritual organizations as well as local communities and families.

Narcissistic abuse is promoted as normal and we are taught not to resist or question it. Those who do speak up and call things out are often humiliated, shamed, and discredited through smear campaigns and character assassinations. The first ones in a family to wake up and call out the abuse are usually met with a similar fate. It's not convenient for the manipulators to have the curtain opened, exposing their game, so they often resort to victim-shaming.

Narcissistic abuse appears to be the thing that's
wrong with the world, and just about everything else fits under
that umbrella. One can only wonder where we go from here as a
society.

The Legacy of Abuse continues to spread until individuals wake up, stand up and speak out the declaration, *it ends with me*. This declaration must then be followed by action, predominantly the act of healing the self. Each individual has a powerful affect on society. It's important not to lose sight of that truth vis-a-vis the overwhelming global problems that we are currently facing.

Your investment in your own self-healing is not selfish but rather self-responsible and it is no small thing.

Every societal change starts within
the hearts and minds of individuals.

What Will You Get Out of This Book?

This book is not about understanding the narcissist, psychopath, sociopath or other narcissistic manipulator. I recommend the books, blogs and videos of HG Tudor[2], Sam Vaknin[3], Dr. George Simon[4] and Dr. Martha Stout[5] for this purpose.

This book is not about how to do No Contact. I highly recommend Kim Saaed's book, *How To Do No Contact Like A Boss*[6] to learn the most important strategy to detach and protect yourself from these kinds of abusers so you can create the space you need in order to heal. If you're co-parenting with an abuser, she teaches you how to modify No Contact to work for you while still keeping yourself as safe as possible.

The purpose of this book is to give those
who have been abused a roadmap out of the suffering
and struggle after narcissistic abuse.

This is a comprehensive, holistic outline of the recovery process so you can measure where you are and where you want to go in the journey of self-healing. If you want to change anything in life, you're going to need to measure it somehow. This structure will help you get to the next level and keep moving forward out of the gravity of the past so you can create a life of peace, joy, meaning and purpose.

I have chosen to use the familiar "you" form in this book as I do in my YouTube videos so that you, as the reader, feel like I'm speaking directly to you. If you're like most of us, you probably felt invisible and ended up craving someone to genuinely see you, hear you and acknowledge that what you went through was real.

This book can apply to any kind of relationship you had with a narcissistic abuser and is not limited to intimate partnerships.

Why Are You Here?

Someone, or perhaps many someones, abused your trust to the point where your entire reality was flipped upside-down and inside-out, leaving you with deep doubts and confusion that threaten your very perception of what's real and what's not.

After months or years of abuse,
your sense of trust is deeply damaged.

You lost trust in yourself, others and likely even the universe/ god. The repetitive experience of fear, terror, deceit, betrayal and loneliness has shaped your life in some major way after narcissistic abuse.

It's normal that your trust has been wounded
and the good news is that it can be recovered.

If the abusive patterns began in childhood, your whole nervous system was programmed to respond in certain ways to people and stimuli in the environment and this will continue unchecked into adulthood until you gain self-awareness around this issue and start transforming your life through the practice of self-care. It was not your fault, however you can change it so you can end the suffering and create the life that you actually want.

When a parent shows one face to the world and an entirely different face to the children — one of cruelty, shaming, criticism, and control alternating with superficial praise and approval or perhaps intermittent acts of kindness, this is deeply confusing to the children who will likely grow up to attract similar types of abusive people because their nervous system recognizes abusive behavior as familiar and normal... or they will turn out to be abusers themselves.

Self-awareness of the familial patterns of abuse often comes as
a result of a wake-up call caused by one or many abusive adult
relationships with intimate partners, friends,
co-workers, bosses, neighbors, family members, etc.

I often hear from clients (and I had the same revelation myself) that once they figured out what was happening and educated themselves on the patterns of narcissistic abuse, they realized that it had permeated their entire life. In other words, if you found yourself in abusive adult relationships, you were likely always surrounded by this toxic dynamic in one form or another.

Every now and then I meet a client who assures me they didn't come from a family of origin with these abusive patterns. Most of them end up telling me down the road that they finally broke through the denial and realized it was always there, perhaps just a lot more covert than what they had experienced with another abuser who woke them up as an adult. It's really hard to accept that one or both of your parents are abusers. Parents are the people who were most supposed to love, support and protect you.

I believe I have seen some clients who truly didn't grow up in an abusive environment. I was curious if there were any commonalities between them. One day I heard Sandra L. Brown[7], author, psychotherapist and founder of The Institute for Relational Harm Reduction & Public Pathology Education, state in an interview that these individuals often went through some kind of devastating loss (i.e. a divorce or the death of someone dear) just before they met a psychopath who preyed upon their vulnerability.

I started asking the clients without a family history of abuse if they had experienced a major loss or something that made them feel very vulnerable right before meeting the abuser. All of them said yes. In most cases it was that someone dear to them had recently died. In a few cases there was an early loss or abandonment of a parent in childhood and then as an adult a life-changing event causing a sense of vulnerability such as moving to a new place and feeling lonely, which preceded the abusive relationship.

This book is relative for people who grew up in a narcissistically abusive family as well as those who didn't but later found themselves in an adult relationship with a narcissistic abuser. If you're still not sure in which category you fit, I believe this book can help you too.

If you've read *Psychopath Free*[8] by Jackson MacKenzie, which I highly recommend, you saw the patterns of narcissistic abuse clearly which is so helpful to recognize what happened to you. Just as the abuse has certain patterns that are similar, the healing process also has similar patterns.

I want to outline some key concepts here before we dive into the journey of self-healing.

The Trauma Bond

Whether it starts in childhood or more recently in adulthood, a trauma bond is formed between the target and abuser. This is also known as the Stockholm Syndrome, the betrayal bond and insane loyalty. Dr. Patrick Carnes' book *The Betrayal Bond*[9] is a fantastic resource on this topic.

The Stockholm Syndrome is a condition that causes hostages to develop a psychological alliance with their captors as a survival strategy during captivity.[10]

The same psychological survival strategy develops in the target of abuse as a result of the intermittent cruelty, harassment, intimidation or forms of covert abuse like little digs, gaslighting, the Silent Treatment or withholding affection, mixed in with acts of perceived kindness.

The trauma bond explains why onlookers can sometimes recognize the abuse and feel disgust toward the abuser while the target could still love and defend the abuser. The loyalty of a trauma bond defies all logic.

It is important to note that the target of abuse is not stupid.

The trauma bond is not a rational or intellectual concept. It appears to be caused by subconscious survival mechanisms built into the primal human brain and nervous system.

There are four characteristics that cause the Stockholm Syndrome[11]:

1. Belief that the abuser can and will kill you (even metaphorically i.e. killing your sense of self)

2. Isolation from perspectives other than the abuser's (you lose your sense of reality and only subscribe to the abuser's reality)
3. The belief that escape is impossible (when you feel like there's no way out you develop learned helplessness)
4. Perceived acts of kindness from the abuser (when you confuse these with genuine care)

The dissolution of the trauma bond happens during a turning point in Stage Two, at the Second Threshold. Until that point you may still feel irrational loyalty and love for the abuser or still be holding onto the hope that you can have a relationship with them without consequences to your wellbeing and/or that they'll change after seeing the wrong of their ways.

During Stage One and the earlier parts of Stage Two, you may notice that you come in and out of denial about the truth of the abuse. You may consciously know that you've been abused for some time before the subconscious denial finally shatters.

The visceral acceptance of the truth is what inevitably dissolves the trauma bond.

This will happen spontaneously during a moment of breakdown/breakthrough, however you can be working in that direction by relentlessly facing the truth as often as possible and avoiding the addiction to indulge in the fantasy/illusion of what you want to believe in i.e. that the abuser will change, the relationship will go back to the "good times," etc.

The Recovery Process

While each of our paths is unique, there are commonalities to the recovery process and it's helpful to have a roadmap from someone familiar with the terrain.

The nature of the self-healing journey is abstract and non-linear. It's not exactly a circle, rather more of a spiral. Healing and transformation take place in layers and octaves.

The journey gets so much better after the really heavy stuff is cleared. For the purposes of writing this book, I will put the stages in chronological order. As you apply these concepts to your life, notice how it flows similarly yet not always in exact linear order.

You might notice that you stayed stuck at a particular point and maybe even returned to earlier stages for a while before moving forward. Don't beat yourself up for this. These are tough lessons to resolve and integrate after the devastation of abuse. I repeated Stage One and early Stage Two many times with different abusers before finally crossing the Second Threshold and breaking the trauma bond to the original abuser in my life.

Keep in mind that this is a complex process. You could be surviving in one area of your life but still feeling victimized in another area or even thriving in some aspects.

Measuring which stage you're in is like measuring brainwaves. When instruments measure a theta brainwave frequency it doesn't mean all the brainwaves are in theta. Various brainwave frequencies can be present, but it means the dominant frequency is theta.

The same goes for the stages of recovery. You are predominantly in one stage at a given time yet you'll have parts of your life and awareness in other stages. You'll also likely be going through multiple transformations in your life at the same time and you may be in a different stage in each of those areas of your life.

It's important to understand that leaving the abusive person and educating yourself about abuse is not the same as healing.

Often people want to believe this is true. What usually happens in those cases where the person doesn't do the inner work to heal is a repetition compulsion. This is when the person endures more abusive experiences until the underlying internal patterns created by the abuse are noticed and healed through the self-care work of Stage Two.

Time alone will not do the healing for you.
You actually have to do the work.

Markers of Change

Document your progress so you can measure it and validate yourself. I highly recommend to journal during your recovery. It will help you to weave pieces of your journey together. You will feel validated and a sense of accomplishment as you look back and notice how far you've come.

The Ego

I want to clarify the connotation of this word as I will use it in this book. The ego doesn't necessarily imply self-centeredness, though it can get out of balance that way. The ego is a part of the human psyche that is necessary for survival in our world.

The ego is an individual identity that provides the differentiation between self and other. It assigns labels and definitions of what we experience in life. The ego is based on separation, which is only one layer of our human being, based in our 3D world, yet it's an important part of being able to function in this world.

Your ego also got badly wounded from the abuse. You lost your sense of self. You became someone you are not to survive and get by and maybe you don't even remember who you are any more. That's okay. You have the opportunity to reinvent yourself now.

Your ego is either going to be your greatest ally
or your biggest obstacle in this self-healing process.

The ego is based in fear. For this reason, the ego is where your biggest obstacles to healing (and life in general) dwell. Because of this fear, the ego is reluctant to change. When it senses annihilation (i.e. of beliefs and concepts that it's attached to), the ego rebels and doubles down. It kicks and screams. The ego doesn't go down without a fight.

Since it's necessary to human life, we don't want to kill the ego. Instead we need to tame it. I find it's best to approach the ego with a lighthearted sense of humor to soften its grip. As my 75 year old adoptive mom and I say, sometimes it's necessary to tell the ego, "Back it up, bitch!"

Being humble is the ability to put your ego aside and see your ugly stuff so you can change it. A person who lacks humility is either unable to see his or her ugly stuff or able to see it but refuses to change it because they would rather believe they're right or in control. A person who lacks humility is too proud to change and therefore not growing. This is often the case of the abuser.

The opposite of humility is pride. Pride has a way of laughing in your face. When life offers you an opportunity to be humbled and make a necessary change, go ahead and put your ego aside so you can grow. It is not easy but it is worth it!

Growth is a choice.

There are opportunities for growth around every corner. Carl Jung wrote, "I am not what happened to me. I am who I choose to become." Years ago when I first read that quote I thought it said chose, as in past tense. Later I realized it's choose, as in the present tense. You didn't choose to be hurt or abused and it wasn't your fault. However, you are continually choosing who you are now by how you show up in every moment and how you deal with the cards that are dealt to you in life. The abuse wasn't your choice. However, your self-healing now is entirely your choice. It's not fair what happened to you. It's not fair you were hurt so much. Life is unfair. You can either sit around and complain about it or you can get back up and invest that energy in your recovery. The choice is yours.

Be willing to set aside your ego and ask for help from caring people along the way, yet recognize that no one can do it for you. Ultimately it's you doing the work to heal yourself. Other people, even professionals, can only nudge you, open the door and point the way.

Self-honesty

The start of self-love is self-honesty. Be as honest with yourself as you can while you read this book and as you go forward in your journey.

Part of being honest with yourself is about not gaslighting yourself. Gaslighting is when one person uses covert aggressive tactics to control the perception of reality of another person leaving them to believe they're going crazy. This is a common tactic used in narcissistic abuse.

After months and years of gaslighting by an abuser,
your own mind can start doing this to yourself.

Notice when you're fooling yourself into believing something you want to believe (fantasy) vs. what's actually in front of you (reality). Notice where you're subscribing to the reality of abusers and thinking you're the crazy one instead of listening to what you know is true even though you may be the only one who sees it. This self-honesty practice is a powerful way to support your sanity after all the gaslighting.

Denial is the most primitive human defense mechanism and it's another way you might be avoiding your truth. When we face awful truths that we don't want to accept, we go first to denial. It's a subconscious thing that takes over.

Later in a (perhaps momentary) state of lucidity you might realize just how in denial you were. I often hear people say, "I know I'm probably in denial about this but…" Our conscious mind often realizes how in denial we are subconsciously but it's the subconscious where the majority of the mind's power exists.

If you want to heal, you must confront these defense mechanisms through self-honesty and relentlessly forcing yourself to face the truth. Eventually you will break through the denial.

Organization of the Book

This book is organized into three parts, the three stages of the self-healing journey after narcissistic abuse:

Stage One: Victim (Powerless)

Stage Two: Survivor (Empowered)

Stage Three: Thriver (Actualized)

Each stage has hallmark emotions, behaviors, feelings, beliefs and perspectives that you'll find in The Common Markers chapter of each stage. These chapters will help you figure out in which stage you currently are and how the next stage differs from where you are now.

The Work chapter is an outline of the key elements of self-healing work that take place within that stage in order to get to the next level and keep moving forward. This is a roadmap of the work that takes place in each stage but it's not a how-to guide. For more information on the nitty-gritty of the self-care work, I recommend the how-to audio and video courses available on my website: Fundamentals of SANA (beginner, Stage One — this course is FREE when you enter your name and email on the homepage), 12-Week SANA Audio Series (intermediate, Stage One and early Stage Two) and the Self-Care Mastery Course (advanced, Stage Two).

In The Rite of Passage chapters I am drawing a parallel between the three stages of recovery from narcissistic abuse and the three stages of Joseph Campbell's Hero's Journey[12], a mythological rite of passage describing the archetypical patterns of human transformation. These chapters include anecdotes from my personal journey as examples to make it relative.

"It is the template of the hero/heroine who goes on an adventure and in a decisive crisis wins a victory and comes home changed/ transformed."[13]

This journey is often represented in epic adventure movies. In real life, the "hero" of the journey isn't a special, chosen someone as in the movies. Rather it is the human journey of transformation, the journey that we are all invited to participate in.

There are three parts and twelve steps in this journey. The human mythology — my story, your story, all of our stories can fit into this template. You could apply it to just about any life transformation that you are going through. I've noticed how this journey happened multiple times during my life, for each major transformation that I've been through, and it continues. As one cycle ends, another begins.

Christopher Vogler[14], writer and guide for Hollywood screenwriters, was inspired by Campbell's work and later came up with the twelve corresponding phases of the emotional journey — the inner journey paralleling the outer adventure. I've woven his emotional phases through the twelve steps of The Rite of Passage because I found this helpful to provide another layer of understanding for each stage of healing. These corresponding twelve emotions and phases of the adventure journey appear in bold text in The Rite of Passage chapters.

I've also added in my own names for each of the twelve phases of the self-healing journey after narcissistic abuse to make the transformations even more specific to our work. You will also find those in bold text.

Remember the journey is a process.
Honor the nature of the process.

It will take some time and it will be well worth your investment in your healing. Have compassion and patience with yourself and others on the journey.

STAGE ONE

Victim Stage
Powerless
Discovery & Awareness

Chapter 1
Summary of Stage One

Stage One starts with Discovery & Awareness. This is the point where you somehow come across a keyword online or a person who mentions a keyword to you, that sends you down the rabbit hole of information seeking.

This discovery of information is the start of the journey of self-healing after narcissistic abuse.

In this first stage of recovery after narcissistic abuse, you go from pretending everything is okay to discovering a horrible truth that you don't want to face. As a result of that truth, your whole life gets flipped upside down and inside out. Your world gets rocked and nothing will ever be the same. You'll probably want to deny it and go back into the comfort of denial.

Once you figure out what's wrong and the house of cards is falling down, you must rebuild a foundation of safety before you can progress further in the healing path. After recognizing the abuse, you're likely left feeling unhinged and unstable, deeply confused and desperately looking for solid ground to stand on. There are so many unanswered questions.

It can even feel like if one more thing goes wrong, you just don't know if you can keep it together any more. Your emotions are intense and all over the place or completely numb. Maybe you even go back and forth between emotional intensity and numbness. These intense symptoms are the reason why it's so important to rebuild a sense of physical and emotional security and stability in Stage One.

The most important thing to learn in early Stage One is that it wasn't your fault.

Let that be your mantra until you cross the First Threshold. The abuse was never your fault. Maybe you kept trying to fix things but it just wasn't working and on top of that, the narcissistic abuser blamed you for it. Keep repeating the mantra to yourself anytime you start blaming yourself for the abuse, or for the relationship not working out, or for feeling like you're not good enough. Keep facing the truth that it wasn't your fault in order to help yourself dissolve the cognitive dissonance and denial so you can release the self-blame and toxic hope, and keep moving forward.

Some people never leave Stage One and remain in the victim state the rest of their life. There are two kinds of victims: 1) the ones who either don't realize that they're victims of abuse or they do realize but can't yet find their way out and 2) the ones who use victimhood as a form of extracting narcissistic supply by preying upon the pity or compassion of others and manipulating others into taking responsibility for them and their problems. Be very careful with the second category of people.

In Stage One you'll also learn a lot more about what you're capable of. By the time you graduate from this stage you'll have taken the reigns of your destiny back in your hands. You will realize that you and only you have 100% responsibility over your life from now on. This shift in self-perspective creates an immediate relief from your previous overwhelming sense of helplessness and powerlessness.

This is essentially the stage where you take your power back.

When you cross the First Threshold, you are no longer a victim. You become a survivor.

Chapter 2

The Common Markers of Stage One

- emotions are intense and all over the place and/or emotions can be numb
- addictions can get worse (drugs, alcohol, food, porn, sex, gambling, shopping, fantasyland, workaholism, etc.) often driven by a desire to numb or escape the intense feelings
- feeling out of control over your life
- anger and hostility, maybe even aggression toward the abuser, toward those who don't want to listen to you and/or those who remind you of the abuser in some way
- repetition compulsion (the past keeps repeating itself through one abusive relationship after another and/or going back to the same source/s of abuse)
- possible dependency on an abuser (could be an ex, a parent, a boss, etc. for financial, emotional, housing or other needs)
- frequent dissociation (where you zone out or check out of your body in order to not feel the pain then you don't remember what happened and why you're missing time)
- dread attacks (an indescribable, overwhelming feeling out of the blue that you're going to die or something is going to go really wrong, often coming on like a tidal wave and paralyzing the body)
- panic attacks (intense fear experienced in the body in various ways such as as difficulty breathing, chest tightness, heart palpitations, sudden coldness/shivering to the bone, sudden heat attack, even feeling like you're going to die)
- anxiety (an underlying, almost constant low-grade sense of fear, often significantly exacerbated in social situations, unfamiliar situations and/or around triggers)
- feeling unsafe (in your home, in your body, in your thoughts or feelings, and/or in the world in general)

- neglecting hygiene and personal needs (maybe you don't want to shower or get out of bed for a period of time, or you let your health issues go, or you don't want to eat, hydrate or exercise) usually caused by a sense of worthlessness and helplessness
- period/s of non-functioning in the world (not able to manage work, bills, responsibilities and/or friends/social relationships, etc.)
- depression (you might feel like everything is awful and it will never get better, maybe you're spending a lot of time in bed or on the sofa tuning out from life in some way with no desire to do what you used to love)
- you likely feel a very limited reality of possibilities and choices (you'll hear negative self-talk like "I can't" and "it's not possible for me")
- frozen in the past (every day and initially maybe all day long, you're rehashing the events of the past, often to the point of obsession, and it feels as if it were still happening)
- pessimistic and/or apathetic about the future
- feelings of helplessness, powerlessness and hopelessness (these three feelings are the dark triad of the victimhood programming caused by abuse, which may continue to a lesser degree through early Stage Two)
- intense shame and feelings of worthlessness (you will likely feel like you're flawed, defective, inferior, unworthy, somehow not good enough and these feelings can be extreme enough at times to convince you that you don't even have the right to exist)
- feeling like it's all your fault (it's not your fault but the abuser taught you this false belief so you would stay in contact, keep trying to fix things, and stay stuck in the abuse cycle)
- heavy sense of fear, obligation and guilt towards the abuser
- desperately seeking answers, playing detective 24/7
- deeply injured sense of trust in yourself, others and/or the universe
- you might feel a sense of relief in a way upon learning the truth about the abuse and betrayal, however it's still incredibly painful and difficult to face
- disorienting confusion ("is it really abuse?" and "is s/he abusive or am I overreacting?") and cognitive dissonance (you'll find

yourself going back and forth in your mind between "it's okay, it's not okay" and "they're abusive sometimes but sometimes they're really nice and they have these redeeming qualities, so maybe they aren't so bad")
   - living in an illusion/fantasy/delusion and wanting so badly to believe in it, mixed with occasional moments of lucidity of the truth
   - brain fog (this makes it really hard to think clearly, increasing the confusion and indecision)
   -abuse amnesia (you might block out periods of your childhood or even recent memories of abuse because your brain couldn't process into long-term memory the reality of the trauma in the moment in order to survive)
   - insomnia and restless sleep, nightmares at times, waking multiple times a night and difficulty falling back asleep
   - existential exhaustion (you may find yourself so tired at times that you have no energy for anything, even what you used to love doing, and you just don't know how to go on in life)
   - irrational loyalty to the abuser (the mandate of silence caused by the abuse plus the trauma bond makes it so hard and scary to speak your truth, so you may be hiding the facts from others — and even yourself, in order to protect the abuser)
   - you might go back to the abuser many times (the average is seven times!)
   - you're possibly frustrating or annoying friends and family by talking incessantly about it or going back to the abuser after they tried so hard to help you get out
   - maybe you find yourself buying courses and books but not doing or reading them, or maybe you're asking for advice but not taking it
   - loss of sense of self and sovereignty (it's like you don't even know who you are any more and you're looking to others to define you and validate you because you're used to being controlled in that way)
   - even after you leave the abuser, it's like you're still living in the trauma due to the constant triggering and flashbacks (random things happen reminding you subconsciously of the abuse, bringing up intense emotions and feelings of the past, sometimes seeing it all as if you were reliving the events)

- devastated self-esteem (you feel really bad about yourself and this is part of the vicious circle keeping you trapped in the abuse cycle and/or accepting abuse from new abusers)
- terrifying vulnerability at times (this can also set you up to be an ongoing target of abuse by predators who sense your vulnerability like a shark smells blood a mile away)
- a rescue fantasy (waiting/wanting for someone to rescue you and this will reinforce your sense of helplessness and powerless, likewise this fantasy keeps you repeating the cycle of abuse with predators that pretend to be rescuers)
- stalking the abuser (online or through in person drive-bys wanting to know what they're doing and who they are with, looking for answers to make sense of things)
- isolation (physical and emotional — you may not feel like going out and being around people because you need some time alone to process and heal, and when you do share with others you might feel like they just don't get it or worse yet they might blame you for it, leaving you feeling even more alone)
- self-sabotage (after you leave the abuser you may find you're punishing yourself in a similar way to how they punished you, like maybe you block your success and joy in order to feel safe as you learned to do with the abuser in order to avoid punishment)
- alternating between self-pity and self-hatred is very common
- when you're stuck in Stage One for years, this means you are resisting growing out of the victimhood (when you realize that it wasn't your fault what happened AND you can do something about it now by taking 100% self-responsibility for your choices now and moving forward, that is where you cross the First Threshold and move into Stage Two)

Stage One symptoms requiring immediate professional help by a licensed psychotherapist, suicide hotline or other local authority:

- self-harm/self-destruction (in some cases you may feel so devastated and out of control that you want to hurt yourself in some way i.e. cutting, impulsive risk-taking, severe addictions or overdoses, etc.)

- suicidal ideation (you may find yourself thinking about suicide whether or not you have a plan or intention to carry it out)

- feeling like your life is in danger (you may be threatened, intimidated, stalked or assaulted by the abuser)

Chapter 3

The Work of Stage One

Stage One is when your whole life gets flipped upside down upon discovering a new truth. This is where the journey of self-healing begins.

Start with the Foundation

The start of the self-healing work of Stage One is about rebuilding your foundation. You start with your basic needs: food, clothing, shelter, safety. Until you have solid ground to stand on, you won't be able to progress through the healing stages.

It's important not to rush this stage. A house built without a solid foundation will crumble. The penthouse is yours if you want it, just be patient with yourself and recognize that you've got to start from the ground up.

Rebuilding Safety

It's critical to rebuild a sense of safety in your body, thoughts and feelings, with people and in your environment. For some, a Protection Order (AKA Restraining Order or Non-molestation Order) may be necessary. In other cases this can make the situation worse because it can trigger the abuser's aggression. *The Gift of Fear* by Gavin DeBecker[1] is a fantastic book that goes into this topic as well as understanding violent behavior in general.

Part of a sense of safety means getting out from under your abuser's authority. It may not be immediately feasible for you to leave due to financial concerns, children, or other complications. If the abuser is paying for your housing or you're living with him/her, you may want to create an action plan for your independence so you can become the authority of your life. That can mean researching new places to live, gaining financial independence, notifying family or friends who will help you leave and/or squirreling away money somewhere the abuser won't find it for your escape/restart fund.

Create a safe refuge for yourself as soon as possible.

It's necessary to have a safe and comfortable living situation after escaping the abuser. You may need to temporarily stay somewhere for a month or few to get on your feet again and this may entail sacrificing some comforts and preferences in the short-term as you work toward your longer-term goals. If the abuser left your home (or simply had keys to it), you may want to look into protective measures like security, cameras, and at the very least new locks. Don't assume the abuser didn't make another copy of your keys.

There may be immediate issues of physical safety that need to be addressed at this time such as protecting yourself and your living environment. If you called out the abuser for who s/he is, they may turn to violence and aggression.

Not all abusers are physically aggressive. The higher level of intelligence and the more covert that the abuser is, the less likely s/he is to use physical violence. The more covert abusers will often try to convince you that you're crazy so you doubt yourself and stay silent about what happened to you. This kind of psychological aggression is an invisible form of violence.

Sometimes it's helpful to move so the abuser doesn't know where you live and also so there isn't a memory around every corner of the house reminding you of him or her. You might even consider moving to a different city to have a clean start and no longer have to run into the abuser in town or pass by all the places where heart-wrenching memories were made. If you are afraid the abuser will track you down or you just really want to get far, far away you might even consider moving countries.

If moving isn't an option in the near future for you, I would recommend remodeling or at the very least repainting some rooms and rearranging furniture to change the energy. This is also a great time to purge any clutter you don't need and also anything the abuser gave you or left you. Getting that stuff out of your space will help to clear the energy so you can start to feel safer and more distant from the abuser.

No Contact Is Ideal

The sooner you go No Contact with the abuser the quicker you'll be on your way to healing. You can manage the relationship for a period of time with boundaries while you get your ducks in order but you'll be spending so much energy in managing it that you won't be able to fully heal until you're separated and disconnected.

Any contact with the abuser is capable of sucking you back into the denial of the trauma bond. People often remark how unconsciously this process happens. It's similar to how an alcoholic might say that they're going to the bar for one drink, but whatever happened between one and blackout they just don't know. Even one text message from an abuser is capable of having that very same effect on you.

Don't let your present circumstances determine your future. Leave as soon as possible, and that might not be tomorrow. Set a deadline for yourself so you have something to hold yourself accountable to.

Remember there is always a way out.

In the cases of people co-parenting with abusers, No Contact means the absolute most minimum contact possible, just to exchange the kids and only working out details about the kids, nothing personal. Kim Saaed's bestselling book *How To Do No Contact Like A Boss*[2] is very valuable for learning how to do No Contact (as well as modified contact in the case of sharing kids).

Addressing Acute Symptoms

During Stage One, you'll be working to develop greater awareness of your acute PTSD/C-PTSD symptoms and this is where a licensed psychotherapist can be really beneficial and often necessary. During this stage, you'll notice a lot of intruding thoughts, emotions, and feelings as well as consistent anxiety, and perhaps even frequent panic attacks, dread and terror.

Often what happens is these intense symptoms begin
as soon as you get yourself to safety,
once you've left the abuser.

Before you leave the abusive environment, you're mostly just trying to survive moment to moment and your survival mechanisms are stuffing it all down so you can get through it. Expect the floodgates to open after you leave so it doesn't surprise you when it happens. Don't freak out. It's not getting worse. It's just all starting to come up to the surface and this is a necessary part of the healing journey.

After you go through a few rounds of those intruding symptoms surfacing, like the dread or panic attacks and flashbacks, you'll be able to develop new understanding and coping skills for navigating those painful and unwanted experiences.

You may want to start seeking professional help from licensed psychotherapists, coaches, teachers, healers, etc. during Stage One. There's no shame in asking for help. Call around and interview professionals to see if they understand the nature of emotional abuse and if they have experience working with people with PTSD/C-PTSD. If they say no, keep looking. If the professional is educated in such matters but when you're working with them you just don't feel a connection or the support you're looking for, end the relationship as soon as possible and keep looking for a better match. I have worked with many clients who said they were more invalidated, blamed, confused (and in some cases even abused) by therapists than any other abuser in their life. Don't stay stuck in that situation. Remember you can always leave.

*Get immediate professional help if you're thinking about
hurting yourself or someone else.*

In Stage One you're likely going to feel very reactive. This is the time to start learning how to respond in healthy ways versus reacting impulsively to the symptoms and triggers. This is a big part of taking your power back.

Get the acute symptoms managed as soon as possible by learning new self-soothing techniques and coping mechanisms so you can start to function again. In addition to therapy, EMDR, guided meditation, binaural beats, Solfeggio frequencies, thymus gland tapping, EFT, yoga, qigong, acupuncture and other holistic modalities could be really helpful in this process. Do some research and see what most resonates with you then start exploring those paths.

Addressing Self-destructive Habits

You'll become more aware of some of your self-destructive habits (how you get in your own way due to what you went through, also known as self-sabotage) and you can start working on redirecting that energy into healthier outlets.

This is where it's important to address addictions and other unhealthy habits so you can start developing a healthier lifestyle through your daily routine. If you're like most of us, you ended up abandoning (or even abusing) yourself to some degree during the abusive relationship and that's why it's so important to turn this around in Stage One.

There can be a lot of shame around these things. Sometimes it's good to say the words out loud so it starts losing power over you. If you aren't ready to talk to anyone else about your addictions or bad habits, then start by journaling. Notice when you sabotage yourself and how you're hurting yourself. Notice how the way you're treating yourself was taught to you by an abuser. Recognize what's got to go so you can move forward instead of holding yourself back.

Learning New Skills & Mindsets

Stage One is also about learning new life skills and perspectives while increasing your inner strength. You'll be starting to seek deeper understanding and working on your personal growth plan. You'll start researching and educating yourself on what happened, the nature of narcissistic abuse, the possible disorder of the person who abused you, etc. You might even get a little obsessed with learning as much as you can. This is quite normal and helpful in this stage.

During Stage One you'll reach the point where you can put the label on the abuser as well as many of the abuser's covert and/or overt manipulative behaviors. You'll start learning the lingo of narcissistic abuse like gaslighting, hoovering, triangulation, devaluation, idealization, discard, scapegoat, golden child, minimization, blame-shifting, guilt-tripping, couching, mobbing, smear campaign, flying monkeys, etc. You'll be able to start categorizing intense emotional experiences with technical words.

This labeling and articulation of the problem starts to diffuse the emotional charge from the experience.

Being able to name it and knowing that it's "a thing," is one of the first reliefs you might feel during this journey. Being able to articulate the problem and put the label on the abuser is key to setting yourself off the hook from the false belief that the abuser likely installed in your mind that it's all your fault.

It's not your fault.

The abuser is the one with the problem. Putting the label on the abuser also starts to dissolve the cognitive dissonance, the excruciating confusion of going back and forth between "s/he loves me, s/he loves me not."

Creating an Action Plan

Start with creating a morning routine, a plan for the first 30-60 minutes of your day after you wake up. Include breakfast, some movement like a walk or stretching, and something inspirational or motivational like music or listening to uplifting speakers online.

Your morning routine will set the tone of your entire day.

Spend this time on YOU, not anyone else. That means not going to your inbox or social media where you will get swept up into everyone else's agendas. If you are a parent, you'll need to schedule this time before your kids wake up.

During Stage One, you're creating a foundational plan for your self-healing journey.

It's important to figure out: 1) Where you are and 2) Where you want to go.

It's like programming a GPS, you have to know both parameters in order to get anywhere. Without one of those parameters, there won't be any forward movement. It's okay that you can't see too far in the future yet, you can keep adjusting your course as you learn and discover new things.

In order to take off on this journey of self-healing, you've got to get some structure in your external physical environment (home and body) as well as your internal environment (thoughts, feelings, emotions, beliefs, and habits).

Create a plan of action for your daily hygiene, nutrition, hydration, movement, and sleep. Whiteboards can be really helpful for planning your meals, daily/weekly tasks, and holding yourself accountable to them. Using a digital calendar to schedule blocks of time for self-care activities on your computer and synching it with your phone reminders is also really helpful.

Add to your plan tending to any injuries or illnesses that may have happened as you escaped the abusive situation. Psychosomatic illnesses and injuries are very common due to the intense stress of the abuse. Get help from professionals when you need it.

Start tapping into your inner and external resources. When the shit hits the fan, it's an excellent opportunity to become more resourceful. You have within you everything you need yet you may want to get help from professionals who can often see what you can't and they can help nudge you toward your path of inner healing.

Safety in Places & People

Avoiding certain places and people may also be necessary in the initial stages of recovery from abuse when you're feeling vulnerable so you don't have to face all the triggers and memories until you get stronger. Later in the recovery process you can reclaim these spaces. During Stage One it's best to give yourself the time to heal first.

Cutting ties with people who still have contact with the abuser is often necessary to protect your peace and sanity. Many of those people can become "flying monkeys," doing the abuser's bidding whether consciously or unconsciously.

You might find yourself quite isolated during this stage as you're realizing who the other toxic people in your life are and you're starting to cut them out.

You may find that you also want a lot of alone time to work things out in your mind and feel your emotions without pretending like everything is okay. This isolation in the early stages is normal and usually necessary to support your healing.

Lean into the discomfort of feeling lonely and you'll learn that it's not so bad.

It's actually much easier to be alone and lonely than with people who you feel lonely around. Facing this sense of loneliness and getting comfortable with it is key to no longer accepting toxic people in your life just because you don't want to feel alone.

Figure out who of your family and friends are safe, meaning who is there to really support you and validate you versus who is there to undermine you, confuse you, blame you and invalidate or minimize your perceptions of reality and the abuse that happened.

Once you start talking about the abuse you'll find out quickly who is supportive and who is not.

People who are in denial and won't hear your truth are not part of your support network and they are not safe to be around during this critical time. It is very important to understand this or you will continually feel invalidated and/or victim-shamed and this will keep you stuck in a holding pattern of seeking outside validation and feeling unable to move forward without it.

Building a Support Network

It's important to start building your support structure during this stage. The isolation from family and friends that results when others don't "get it" can be devastatingly lonely. This is why many of us turned to support groups online or in person during this stage in order to talk with others who had similar experiences and can validate our stories. This may be the first time you speak your truth.

When you hear the stories of others who went through it, you'll realize that you're not alone and you're not crazy.

It's necessary to exercise caution in all support groups, including religious and spiritual organizations, because such communities often draw in abusive types hiding among the crowd and using the support structure to abuse vulnerable newbies. This is where your discernment of toxic or not comes in. It will take some time to develop this sense of discernment after you've lost your sense of trust.

Don't beat yourself up if you don't recognize the toxicity right away. Sometimes it's very covert. When you look back, notice the moments when your intuition was telling you something was off but you ignored it. Now you know what to look for. Every time you interact with another toxic person you will learn more about how they behave and how you react to it. Instead of putting yourself down, recognize the valuable lesson you learned, helping to grow your wisdom and awareness, then integrate that moving forward.

It's important to hang out with people who are patient and compassionate with you during this process. If people are telling you to "just get over it" or "just let it go" when you're in the early stages of recovery, it's going to feel really invalidating and could cause you to beat yourself up or self-doubt more than you already are. If people are blaming and shaming you for where you're at, don't hang out with them.

What you most need at this point are people
in your life who believe your story
and those who can show you
by their example that healing is possible.

Hang out with people like that and your healing will be expedited because we become like those we spend time with.

Redefining Your Ego & Sense of Self

You'll start to strengthen your sense of self during this stage. Essentially you're restructuring your ego/identity, which was wounded by the experiences of your past. You likely got confused about who you are, what was real and what wasn't, what was yours and what was the abuser's responsibility or what was really you and what was you emotionally reacting to extreme situations.

You need to redefine your identity because your previous self was
based on the role the abuser created for you and you likely gave up
a lot of yourself in the process.

In Stage One, you'll start to discover more about who you really are and you'll start creating a new and stronger sense of self. In the process of redefining who you are, you're also redefining what is your reality.

It's not your fault. This is a key belief system that you'll be working to integrate into your subconscious during Stage One. Previously you had likely blamed yourself or felt responsible for the abuse of the past or the relationship not working out because abusers generally do an excellent job of convincing the target of that.

Once you fully realize that it's not your fault, you can let go of your ego's attachment to trying to fix it or hoping it can be fixed, as well as the pressure and blame you've been putting on yourself, a burden that is not yours to carry. This reframing is very important so you can reinvent yourself and leave behind the script the abuser taught you.

New Boundaries

You'll be working to set and enforce new boundaries to protect yourself during Stage One. Boundaries can be physical in terms of protecting your body and environment from certain people or situations. Boundaries can also be mental and emotional. These are trickier to see because they are invisible yet very important.

The most foundational boundary to start putting into place in Stage One is the boundary of NO.

Start looking at where in your life you need to say NO. Where are you leaking energy from? Where are you giving too much and not receiving reciprocity in return? Where are you putting others' needs before your own? Start saying NO more often.

It's uncomfortable at first, especially when you face the backlash from toxic people who are upset that they're no longer getting what they want from you. Stand your ground and it will get easier and easier. This may be the first time in your life that you give yourself permission to say NO. Perhaps since childhood you were conditioned to believe that you didn't have that right and if you did express your NO, you were likely punished. Now it's time to start re-wiring that programming by giving yourself permission to say NO when you need to.

Start noticing how others are affecting your thoughts and emotions. If you don't like how you feel after hanging out with someone or the thoughts that they planted in your mind with the words they said, start drawing new boundaries to not let that stuff in. You might still be thinking of things abusers told you a long time ago based on their reality paradigm and that's another opportunity to practice mental boundaries. Create a mantra that you use to draw the mental boundary instantly when needed.

That's not my reality!

Boundaries can also be financial. Maybe you need to draw the line and stop supporting an abusive person who was playing your heart strings with their pity-ploys. You might also need to stop accepting financial gifts from abusers who are using that money to control you.

Spiritual boundaries are also important, especially when the relationship had a religious or spiritual influence in your life. Spiritual abuse can be deeply devastating to your soul. Many spiritual abusers try to manipulate you into giving them what they want and tell you that if you don't fulfill their expectations or if you set any kind of boundary then you're not kind, compassionate or understanding. Don't internalize that stuff. Remind yourself who you are. Many covert spiritual abusers misdirect you with blame-shifting phrases like, "it seems like you're being triggered so let's talk about where that's really coming from," when that person is actually abusing you.

Own your reality.

Abusers hate your boundaries because it means they can't get what they want so expect them to be upset when you start setting new limits on what you will and will not tolerate. Stand strong and enforce your boundaries.

In most cases, it will get worse before it gets better.

That is exactly when you need to stand strong and enforce your boundaries. If you go back on your boundaries, the abuser will understand you don't mean it and they'll keep taking advantage of you.

Understand that you have the right to have boundaries and this does not mean you are not a compassionate person. Compassion has to have limits too. Start by first asking if you're being compassionate with yourself.

Stage One work is NOT about dealing with childhood memories and an in depth exploration of the past. That takes place in Stage Two. Before you open up that can of worms, it's important to set up your foundation of safety, support and basic self-care otherwise it will be too overwhelming.

The Jump from Stage One to Stage Two

Judith Herman describes the transition from Stage One to Stage Two as, "Once a sense of safety, stability, good self-care and the ability to adequately regulate emotions has been achieved, stage two may be moved on to." She wrote in *Trauma & Recovery*, "No single, dramatic event marks the completion of the first stage."[3]

In terms of recovering from the trauma of narcissistic abuse specifically, I agree that Stage One requires creating a sense of safety, support, groundedness and important foundational self-care practices including balancing intense emotions and regulating self-destructive behaviors while setting new boundaries. However, I do see a dramatic event that marks the completion of this first stage. It doesn't look outwardly dramatic but internally it's a massive shift that changes everything.

I believe there is a clear and tangible upliftment from the victim into the survivor state. I can see this turning point in my own life and in those I've worked with. Crossing The First Threshold between

Stage One and Two is reflected in Joseph Campbell's Hero's Journey[4] when the hero fully commits to the transformation. In terms of the self-healing journey after narcissistic abuse, this threshold is the point where you take 100% self-responsibility for your life and choices now and moving forward.

Chapter 4

The Rite of Passage: Stage One
Separation & Invitation

In the beginning of Stage One, you're in your everyday life, your **(1) Ordinary World**[1], going about your days. You identify with a certain way of being and living. You are aware of some of your capabilities, talents and dreams and you have a certain outlook on life.

At the beginning of Stage One, you're **Living in Denial**. You're in the illusion, fantasy, idea of what your life could be but you're largely unaware of the reality that you're actually living in. On the daily you're stuffing away your feelings to get by. You're minimizing and invalidating yourself, and possibly desperately seeking validation from others but worse yet there may not even be many others to get validation from.

Deep down in your soul, there's some kind of restless, gnawing feeling that there's something missing or something wrong but since you don't know what it is yet, you try to pretend that you don't feel it.

You likely feel **Incomplete**[2] in some way. You're not really fulfilled or happy and maybe you kind of want to fix that, but at the same time you don't want to because it seems like such a drag to do anything about it. In this early stage there's a sense of complacency. If you're somewhat honest with yourself in this phase, perhaps you'll notice that you have an unresolved desire in your heart and an unexpressed song in your soul. At this point you've still got a limited self-awareness of your wound and that's exactly what's blocking you.

At first everything is seemingly "fine." Yet underneath the surface, some part of you senses that you're pretending everything is okay. You're probably living in a state of ignorance, denial, and rationalizations though you're largely unaware of that yet. You have a rationalization for everything that you're allowing in your life and you're comfortable with that because it feels normal.

Back in 2014, I was living in Portland and going about my days. I was existing but struggling and in deep denial. My boyfriend of eight months was a covert narcissist, though I didn't want to believe it. At the time, I had no idea that this pattern had been repeating with every significant other that I had after high school, not to mention some bosses, co-workers, friends and neighbors. I was also clueless to my own codependency patterns and the C-PTSD that had been with me probably my whole life. I just thought I had bad luck in relationships because I wasn't good enough.

So there I was, contenting myself with his meager breadcrumbs of love and his generous yet empty promises for the future. When we were together we mostly had fun and that was mostly because I was so accommodating to his needs, his schedule, his desires and whims. I never knew how long he would stay. Maybe a few hours, maybe just an hour or two. Every time I saw him my whole body was in a state of tension bracing for the moment when he would say he had to go. I would hold my breath every time he moved because I was always expecting him to make his slide toward the door and I never knew when he would be back.

Every time he left quickly and abruptly I couldn't focus on anything I wanted to work on. My head would spin and the rest of the day would disappear into the oblivion. I was trying to make my holistic coaching business work but failing miserably. I had so much free time but it was useless due to my inner state of worthlessness.

Deep down I knew I wanted to do more with my life but I didn't know how to go about it and I didn't really believe in myself either. I knew I wanted to make a difference in people's lives and I knew it had something to do with holistic healing and coaching. I had been struggling at the business side of it for a decade already. I couldn't define my niche audience because I wasn't yet in contact with my own core wound.

I would see him once or twice a week for the little bits of his time that he could dish out to me, and when he was there I would smile, take care of him and pretend to be happy. I would minimize my feelings of sadness and loneliness on the daily. I focused mostly on him and making him happy, and if he was happy I was happy. I would tell my friends how happy I was with that guy and how excited I was about our future. I think I actually believed it at the time. I was hiding from them the truths of the relationship because I was trying to hide it all from myself.

On the surface it didn't look that bad. That made it all the more difficult to articulate to myself what was wrong. There was a subtle, gnawing feeling of restlessness and anxiety that would increasingly creep up to show me how unhappy and unloved I really was. There was no solid ground to stand on in the relationship, just a lot of idealization, promises and other meaningless words that I was hanging on to for dear life.

As the months went on, instead of a growing sense of security and intimacy together as it occurs in healthy relationships, things just got more nebulous and confusing. I was so disempowered I was barely getting by and I depended on my boyfriend to help me financially. It sounded like a good idea at first to accept his help when he so generously offered, but I quickly realized it was a huge mistake. I had given up my freedom in the process.

I had never been dependent on a man before. Usually in relationships I was depleting my resources supporting men. I had no idea how worthless I would feel if I let someone masquerading as a hero, rescue me, because then I felt like I could no longer rescue myself. I was so ashamed of this that I buried it to pretend it wasn't happening. The more the stuffed-down shame grew, the lower my self-worth fell and the harder it was to accomplish anything, even simple tasks. It was a vicious circle keeping me stuck and unable to move forward. I didn't see a way out so it was easier to just pretend everything was okay.

When he was off living his other life, which all along he promised he wanted to leave but never did, I would deal with it by isolating and smoking a lot of weed while binging on Netflix, Facebook, the news, learning online, or taking trainings and courses. I would sometimes lose hours and days running endless circles in my mind while smoking cigarettes at my window and in my secret spots around town, because as a holistic healer I wasn't supposed to be smoking. All around, I wasn't living in integrity with myself. On top of it, I was hiding the pain from myself. I was hiding the truth from myself. I comforted myself in all of these distractions instead of being present and actually feeling the feels. I didn't want to feel it. I didn't even know what *it* was but I knew that it was there.

In this early stage, despite the buried issues that you might be somewhat aware of but mostly pretend don't exist, you're living in your comfort zone and you're oblivious of what's to come.

Then one day it all starts falling apart.

(2) The Disruptive Truth pierces your comfortable denial. You find out something that changes everything. At a deep level you sense something is really wrong in your life and you need to do something about it.

Perhaps it's through a massive betrayal, a cunning deception, a devastating disappointment from someone you love. It could even be an emotional flashback or memory suddenly surging that forces you to face the past and relive it in some symbolic way. However it unfolds, this initiating event causes your psychological defenses to break down.

A new truth is revealed,
leaving you with deep internal conflicts to resolve.

This event is somehow a direct threat to your worldview and way of life. Your peace is disrupted because you can't unlearn what you just found out.

Essentially the seemingly misfortunate turning point event is a cosmic challenge, an invitation to a quest. It's your **Call To Adventure**[3], as Joseph Campbell called it. Something spontaneous (you could even say miraculous in some cases) takes place and you're suddenly catapulted out of your mundane reality. Everything changes on a dime and naturally you feel **Unsettled**[4].

One day my boyfriend came for lunch and told me he was leaving the next day for his daughter's white coat ceremony at her medical school across the country. I was shocked. How did he not tell me this sooner?

At first he rug swept it like it was no big deal, but it was. For some reason I knew this was a big deal.

He said he just forgot about the trip until then, but I knew how much pride he took in his daughter following his footsteps as a physician and I knew he had to have requested the time off work a while in advance so none of that made sense. Then he casually changed his tune and said he thought he mentioned it to me a while back. He didn't. Of course he only had breadcrumbs of time to share with me that day since he needed to pack for the trip.

After he left, I couldn't stop thinking about it, obsessing about it. I spent the rest of the day and night sitting at my window smoking cigarettes and hashing things out in my mind. He superficially apologized via text that night and he said all the right words but it still didn't feel right. Something was really wrong but I couldn't pin-point what it was.

The next day on his way to the airport he did a total

flip-flop, texting me that I needed to get over it and that it's not a big deal. Then he mostly disappeared from communication for a few days. The Silent Treatment. I felt even more desperate for answers.

The day after he left, my dog got attacked by another dog at the park and she was dripping blood from her face. I texted him about it and didn't hear back for over eight hours. Even then, his response was alarmingly unconcerned. The next day I woke up with a gushing nose bleed and giant clots of blood that wouldn't stop for over fifteen minutes. These were signs of the loss of life force energy that relationship was causing to me and my dog.

The last night he was there he started texting again as if nothing happened. I texted him a screenshot of an ad that appeared while I was watching a series online. It was the hotel where we had stayed in Vegas, months before. I was deluding myself that it was a good sign.

He knew how much I love synchronicity. He texted back that he was reading Esquire magazine on the flight out there and he saw the same ad and thought of me. My gut dropped. I just knew he was lying. I couldn't explain how but I just knew. It seems so petty but this was a big deal because it meant something bigger than the little lie about the synchronicity. I couldn't sleep that night wondering what was going on and what I should do about it.

The next morning I went to Powell's to find the current Esquire magazine. I flipped through every page and didn't see the ad. I bought the magazine and took it home to comb through it thoroughly, several more times. *Nada.*

When he got back from the trip, he sat down on my sofa and in the few moments while my back was turned serving something in the kitchen, my dog had bitten and bruised both his forearms. I don't know what he did to elicit that reaction from her but it sure shifted the focus quickly from his inconsiderate actions regarding the trip to a pity-ploy where I was again feeling bad for him and upset at my dog.

We went out to the park to smoke and I gave him a soft-test on his lie. I asked him if he read Esquire for the fashion or articles. He said the articles are great. I asked what kind of articles he read on the flight. He described three of them. Sure enough all three of those articles were in the edition of the magazine I had bought. Not only did he lie to me he also exploited my love of synchronicity, something sacred to me, in order to manipulate my emotions to serve his needs.

In that moment I started having flashbacks of lots of things he said over the eight months we were together. The memories were flying by at light speed while the world around us seemed to shift into slow motion. Then suddenly I had the feeling that just about everything he ever told me was a lie or manipulation to get what he wanted.

Sitting on the park bench with him in that moment, I felt like reality all around me was collapsing like a scene from the movie *Inception*[5]. I was waking up from the illusion I had been living in and it wasn't pretty.

My denial was pierced. I could no longer go back to pretending everything was alright. Yet at the moment it was all so overwhelming and disorienting that I didn't know what to do about it. The thought of having to end it seemed too devastating to face.

After the truth-revealing event, you have a new awareness of what's going on in your life and the need for imminent change even though you might not want to really face it yet. Don't beat yourself up for it, no one really wants to face that stuff. The illusion and fantasy is so much prettier.

The nature of a crisis is a breakdown, then a breakthrough.

Everything falls apart so you can begin rebuilding yourself and your new reality.

The old reality has to collapse so you can experience the new. It doesn't work any other way. The sooner you help yourself surrender to your truth, the better. The longer you fight it and cling to denial, the more you will suffer.

This crisis, whether by divine intervention or a random event, is the catalyst and opportunity for your growth. It sure doesn't look like a blessing in the moment. In fact it looks awful and you probably wish it never happened but it's real.

The sooner you let go of the ego attachments (i.e. trying to change, fix or control the other person's problems, trying to cling to the fantasy/idea of what it could be or what you wanted it to be) that are stopping you from accepting the truth, the quicker you'll be on your way to heal. It's crushing to the ego to accept that it was deceived but this acceptance is necessary to move forward.

Face the ugly truth relentlessly to speed up this process.

The withdrawal from the fantasy is brutal. The fantasy makes you feel a certain way, and that feeling feels so much better than letting yourself feel the reality of the situation and the devastating sense of loneliness and betrayal under the surface.

Why is it so hard to make the decision to walk away from something that's hurting you? The fantasy of what it could be and what it might be or what you thought it would be at the beginning feels so damn good that it keeps you wanting to hang on because maybe just maybe…

As the fantasy is imploding, you're forced to face a dilemma and you're practically forced into change. It's deeply disturbing. You're probably terrified to make the change. Making this decision means that you're acknowledging your world will never be the same.

After that day in the park, I started telling a few friends what was going on. They all agreed that guy was no good for me, which started to solidify the truth in my own mind, overwriting the fantasy and false hope that I had previously been living in. On a walk with an older friend, she mentioned the term "narcissist" again for the first time in about five months. She reiterated that he was the same as the more obvious abusers from the past, *he's just the more sophisticated model.* Later I watched a few videos on YouTube about the topic and it all sounded way too familiar. Every one of the experts said to get away from the narcissist ASAP. But I really wanted to believe that he was the exception. Don't we all?

Somehow I knew that I couldn't just leave him and stay away. I didn't trust myself to follow through and not give into the temptation to see him if he said all the right things, which he was so talented at doing. I knew I had to do something much more drastic or I was doomed to go back to him and repeat the experience. I felt trapped in the financial dependency to him and didn't know what to do to get out. I knew there had to be another way but I didn't know where to start.

That week I heard from my landlord that they had to give up my apartment in a lawsuit, which meant I had to move soon. I figured that was a sign.

My hairdresser out of the blue mentioned she read an article on ayahuasca and asked me if I had ever tried it when I lived in Peru. Ayahuasca had been on my radar for eight years but we never crossed paths. After her reminder, I put on Netflix and watched some documentaries of people's experiences with the plant medicine. Every part of my body and mind told me it was time to go back to Peru and figure it out there.

After some reflection, I decided to put everything I owned into storage and head to Peru for a couple months. My intent was to drink ayahuasca and figure out why I kept attracting narcissists. By this point I was realizing that I'd been in relationships with various shades of narcissists, sociopaths, psychopaths and malignant borderlines for years. They weren't just my intimate partners but also bosses, coworkers, neighbors and friends. I figured there must be something in me that was drawing them in and I wanted to get to the bottom of it.

That was great and all but I still had the problem of *no way out*. I was completely dependent on him financially. I realized how he did that to lock me in and the options to get out looked so slim. The older friend who mentioned the term narcissist suggested that I ask him for money to start my life over. That seemed inconceivable to me. She said this probably wasn't the first time he had to buy his way out and she's probably right about that. Money was his favorite form of control. He had a lot of it and he knew exactly how to apply pressure points with it, all the while making himself look like a hero.

I knew I couldn't directly ask him for money to leave him because that would give him zero control and nothing he wanted. So I pretended like I planned to come back to him after Peru and I mentioned our earlier idea of maybe living together in January after I returned. I'm not proud of that. Essentially that's called counter-manipulation. At the same time it was also partly true because I still had shreds of toxic hope that we could actually be together even though my conscious mind knew it had to end.

Once you're in way too deep with a narcissistic abuser, in many cases you'll have to cut all your losses and run with almost nothing because everything was taken from you. I've done that several times. The other option is to intuitively sense the counter-manipulative move to make that lets you out gracefully with what you need to move on, while giving the narcissistic abuser a sense of control and feeling like they won something they want. That move I only had to make twice in my life. It can be really helpful in dire situations where you don't have access to the financial or other resources that you need to actually leave and you need the abuser to be willing to help. Use this option cautiously.

Looking back now, I accept that I did what I had to do to get myself out of that relationship without having to return to my parents' house where my original abuser was. I knew I had to avoid that at all costs. The idea of going back there felt like death, the death of my soul. Maybe you can relate to having to do things you normally wouldn't do in order to get out of a severe situation.

While I was going to be gone, he was going to lose his driving privileges for a few months due to a DUI so it was going to be very hard for us to see each other anyway. I was almost surprised how easily he agreed that it was best and gave me the money for the trip. Surely he was thinking about not having me around while he enjoyed his other sources of narcissistic supply at work so in a way it was a win/win. The only way to get away from a narcissist by playing their game is to create a win/win situation with the ambiguity of getting back together later because that's exactly what the narcissist wants. They want to know they can have their fun and you'll be there waiting for them when they get bored or their new supply runs dry.

Part of me still had hope that a few months away from him would be his wake up call, encouraging him to change his ways and that maybe we would get a place together when I returned. I didn't know how to exist in Portland if he wasn't in my life. Totally delusional, I know. I needed a total reset.

The covert types are the worst mindfuck. Their sophisticated level of gaslighting is so stealth, well crafted and delivered that it can lead you to truly think you're going crazy. Their mask is so well designed that no one else can see who they really are beyond the superficial charm and eloquence so you feel even more alone and end up doubting your perception of reality. Once you figure out who they really are, you're left not knowing what was real and what wasn't. You wonder if it was all a lie. It's terrifying when you feel like you're losing a grip on your mind and can't distinguish reality from the illusion that you lived in for months or years.

At some level we all probably sense the devastating pain that is coming after the decision to see the truth and accept it, so that's why we avoid it. The first three months of withdrawal from the fantasy are the worst, the first month of which, is practically torturous. If you want to get out of that prison, you have to do the time anyways, so you might as well start now.

If not now, when?

Maybe you really want to do it, you want to change your life, but the problems you're facing feel like too much to handle. You might doubt your capabilities and endurance. How could you have the energy to face the truth and make the necessary changes in your life to support that truth when you're so exhausted already and your self-esteem is so low? How are you going to find the financial resources to start over if you're dependent upon an abuser? It's a very difficult situation that people often find themselves in.

Maybe you're eager to accept the Call To Action but you have crushing fears, doubts and paralyzing second thoughts. You're afraid to fail, afraid of the unknown, afraid of the loneliness that may take place in the process. Maybe someone else even presents you with an invitation to feel doubts and fears when you share with them your excitement about the changes you want to make in your life.

A few weeks later by the time I was leaving for Peru, I had stopped accepting his manipulations and breadcrumbs of love and instead started focusing on me again, as painful as it was.

Starved of the narcissistic supply that he used to get so easily from me, he got desperate to see me. He tried to stop by my apartment unannounced while I was busy packing to make the moving deadline. I didn't answer. He was so injured by this lack of supply and the shock that I actually didn't accommodate his every whim, causing him to escalate the abuse with some nasty words via text. He was unmasking and revealing himself. Eventually even the covert types become overtly abusive when you take away their supply before they're ready to discard it.

He tried to get me to doubt myself, my capabilities and

my perceptions of reality. He tried to guilt-trip and blame me for things not working out. He even tried to stoke my hope, all practically in the same breath.

Even though I hadn't heard of No Contact yet, I knew I had to block him from contacting me so I could clear my head, retain my sanity and summon my inner resources to embark upon the journey ahead.

It's so important to shift your perspective into the openness of new possibilities. The abuser convinces you that there's no way out. Many times I found myself in situations where I didn't see a way out, but it was the negativity paradigm of the abuser keeping me behind holographic prison bars.

The bars don't actually exist but in your mind.

Your mind is either your greatest strength and resource, or it's your worst enemy. It all depends on how you're feeding it. When your situation seems impossible, that is a calling from the universe for you to get resourceful and summon every drop of courage you have in order to survive and move forward.

I have worked with clients who told me they got themselves out of the most seemingly impossible situations long before they found out about narcissistic abuse and without any guidance but their own internal intuition. Your intuition will always help you find the way out if you can get real and trust it, while stopping yourself from trying to see what you want to see instead. When the pain of staying where you are becomes greater than your projection of the pain of the unknown change on the horizon, that is the moment when you will summon your courage to make a brave move forward.

Of course the comfort of home (i.e. denial) looks much better than stepping into the unknown. Some part of you is reluctant at this stage. This is the **(3) Refusal Of The Call**[6]. You are **Resistant**[7] to change at this point. You may even rebel against this idea that you have to change in order to be happy because you feel **Caged by Self-doubt**.

Maybe you're rationalizing your refusal to make the decision so you comfort yourself in false logic. You might realize that you're doing anything and everything to convince yourself not to face the truth. No matter which method you use to pretend it's not happening, at some level, you know that the reveal has already taken place. Life will keep sending you opportunities for repetition compulsion until you wake up and take massive action. Many people get stuck here and go back to the abuser (or a new one) for another round or several. For me this was an entire year of intense lessons in this phase.

By the time my brother and I landed in Peru, I'm sure he was tired of hearing about my ex. A couple weeks after arriving, we went to a retreat to drink plant medicines. Through those experiences and sharing them with my brother, I gained invaluable new clarity and insights. We ended up processing a lot of childhood trauma together and he told me stories about what he experienced with my mom that I didn't even know. With so much still unresolved about the recent relationship, I was only starting to see the truth of who my mother is and how it was all connected. That had to get shelved for the time being.

By the end of our two-month trip, I knew I was never going back to that guy or other abusive people from my past, several of whom had synchronistically contacted me while I was traveling and working on these deep issues. I vowed to never let myself stay in another relationship where I felt the devastating loneliness that I had felt yet stuffed down all my life until that point, which the medicine journeys had made so painfully clear to me.

I decided my next step was to move to Peru indefinitely and work in a retreat with the plant medicines for my own healing and helping others. I realized that the plants don't cure you, rather they hold the mirror for you to see your stuff, which you otherwise haven't been able to see because your mind was caught up in the programming taught to you all your life. What you do with that new awareness is up to you. If you do nothing new, nothing changes. Awareness is not the same as healing. Healing involves integrating that awareness by taking new action accordingly.

And so the universe began to test me on my new vows and revelations. I failed many times before I could figure it out. The school of life can be brutal sometimes but inevitably you learn more there than in any institution of higher learning.

The rest of that year in Peru was like my immersion training in narcissistic abuse. I didn't learn it from a book, a course or a seminar. I learned it through life, through more devastating experiences with several more abusers and manipulators who came across my path. I witnessed a whole spectrum of different forms of abusive types of people. I also met some wonderful, loving people along the way who helped me keep the love and light alive in my heart.

A year after I had arrived, I left Peru running, in tears of defeat and loss, and with no Plan B. I had zero dollars in my bank account. My business partner owed me money yet I knew he wasn't going to pay me. Part of me wanted to stay to fight for what was mine but I also knew that I had to get out of that environment right away because I couldn't be anywhere around those people if I wanted to retain my sanity. I had to ask my parents for money to help me get out of the country. It was the most ashamed and disempowered I had felt in my entire life.

I returned to my parents' house in the Mid-west not sure if I even had it in me to try again. That was the last place I wanted to be. It was the place I most wanted to avoid and I knew once I arrived, it was going to be very, very hard to find the way out and forward. There was no hope left, no light in the distance. I considered giving up at life one last time.

Sometimes the devastating awareness of the truth and the feeling that life as you once knew it is imploding all around you, is so overwhelming that you don't even want to take care of your basic hygiene let alone nutrition and exercise. This inability to function at basic levels of self-care is very common in the early stages of the C-PTSD recovery. Maybe you realize you need to take some time off from life for healing. It's okay to need a time out.

I wasn't capable of functioning for several weeks when I hit the bottom of the bottom C-PTSD crash in October of 2015 at my parents' house. There were many days I couldn't force myself out of bed to shower. There was no reason to. I had no sense of purpose, nothing to live for.

I didn't leave the house. I couldn't face life. I didn't want to see anybody. I didn't want to eat. I didn't want to exercise. Mostly I just wanted to cry, smoke cigarettes and feel bad while rehashing the past over and over, thinking about all those people and how they betrayed me, then beating myself up for letting it happen. Every moment I was awake, I was fighting with them in my mind. Even in my dreams I was fighting the injustice. I was utterly exhausted.

I was still desperately trying to get my former business partner in Peru to pay me the buy out sum he owed me for signing over my half of the business along with everything I had created during the last six months. I had worked for free for six months on the promise of making money when we opened. But even after we opened we didn't get paid because he, the investor, said he had no more money to invest. That was a lie of course. When he decided to make his power move he sat me down to tell me that he was going to invest more money in the business but on the condition that he would take over one hundred percent control. That was the day I decided to leave. He wasn't happy about my decision because he wanted me around to abuse and exploit but none of that was visible on the surface, just his fake eye smile and his feigned concern and compassion when he suggested a possible new career direction for me in the area helping businesses get started and he wanted me to issue something of a public statement where I announced my reason for leaving, that I'm good at setting up businesses but not good at running them. I knew that was a trap not to mention a total lie and projection because as I was working twelve hours a day he was sitting on the patio surfing online or chatting people up. I wanted to be as far away from that character as possible.

Still I gave him everything I had created before leaving, trusting that he would do the right thing and pay me the buy out sum as was written in the legal contract. I was mad at myself that I didn't withhold at least the website access until the money was in my account. I was mad at myself that I trusted yet another person who betrayed my trust.

With each email that I wrote him reminding him that he owed me the buy out money, and his responses with false accusations and utter bullshit reasons why he couldn't pay me yet, my self-esteem was plummeting lower and my sense of helplessness and powerlessness was growing exponentially. Meanwhile I struggled to kill the toxic hope that maybe just maybe he was going to do the right thing and pay me. Rage was boiling in my blood thinking about how someone could do that to someone else and why did I trust him without protecting myself. So much regret. So many tears.

You might also refuse to make this shift into empowerment for a period of time and instead stay wallowing in the suffering, self-doubt and feelings of worthlessness. This decision to take care of yourself is even harder to make when you are living in an abusive environment. You might not see a way out and some people even consider suicide. **Please get professional help from a licensed psychotherapist if you're at this point.**

Stuck at this impasse with life, you might feel like you desperately need guidance, someone to dispel your doubts and fears... Someone to validate you and tell you that it was real what happened to you and that everything is going to be alright... Someone to tell you that you didn't deserve to be treated like that... Someone to tell you what the hell to do now.

Then suddenly one day you'll end up **(4) Meeting a Mentor**[8]. This guide will give you the faith to help you feel **Encouraged**[9] to get going. It's usually a person who comes across your path with exactly the message you need to hear, right when you need to hear it. Nowadays with the internet, this mentor may appear to you online or in person. You might be afraid to trust this person at first. You might be confused and unsure if it's a friend or foe after what happened in the past.

It's important to be able to separate the message from the messenger, the wheat from the chaff.

Your mentor might only come into your life for a brief moment of time to deliver the message and then part ways. The mentor might even be a toxic person who encourages you, however painfully, to grow. Or it could also be the start of a deep, lifetime connection.

The teacher appears when the student is ready, and usually not in the form you're expecting. You will notice that you meet at least one of these mentors during the initiation to every major transformation of your life. The universe is uncanny and helpful that way. It's up to you to recognize the opportunity.

Your mentor is simply a part of your story, they are not your rescuer. Maybe that person saved your life with the faith, information or advice that you needed, but actually, you saved yourself. You made the decision. You did the work. You are your own guru. Don't give away your power to anyone else. Not even a teacher.

The most effective mentors and teachers nudge you with their knowledge and challenges as they point the way through their living example, encouraging you to find your own inner guru — your intuition, your inner knowing. This is empowering.

Powerlessness is the predicament of Stage One until you cross the First Threshold into Stage Two.

Depending where you are in life, the mentors who show up

might try to make themselves the sole authority of your healing and manipulate you in the process. Don't fall for this. I did. I had several of those teachers and went back to feeling like a victim at several points earlier in my life. Inevitably, I learned valuable lessons from them but most of those experiences were really painful and sometimes scary.

A teacher who makes him/herself indispensable to your healing and learning rather than empowering you to do it for yourself, is dangerous indeed. These are often the kinds of narcissistic teachers you'll find in spiritual and religious organizations. I have had several clients and friends tell me stories of well-known spiritual gurus and holistic experts that they were intimately involved with and now recognize as psychopaths and narcissists. The biggest challenge of that kind of abuse is when the rest of the students are still under the spell and they can't see the truth so they defend the abusive teacher causing you to doubt yourself more. Get away from those teachers and their toxic environments ASAP!

Your mentor is someone who believes in you. I like to call this person a soul pilot lighter because sometimes the pilot light of the soul gets extinguished when we go through long, difficult experiences. When another person comes along and believes in you, this encouragement can be the spark **Reigniting Your Soul Pilot Light**. This mentor is your first ally on the journey. In Stage Two, you start to meet more allies.

With your mentor, you start to talk about your predicament and break the silence. Abuse comes with a devastating imposed silence. The wound of not feeling heard is painful and lonely. At this point you start dissolving the burden of the shame by talking about it with someone who validates you and gives you something you need.

In the movies, this is the part where the hero gets some kind of valuable object, information or training from a mentor. That might be true for you. Or maybe through your mentor you discover a new understanding that dissolves the fears and doubts you had. You get something from your mentor that you desperately needed, like encouragement, validation or solidarity, and that gives you a sense of permission and faith to answer the calling and move forward.

During my C-PTSD breakdown in October of 2015, a former client of the retreat where I worked contacted me out of the blue. At first I was nervous to have any contact with him because of his connection with my former business partner. I didn't know if he was a flying monkey. He asked me what happened and why I left. I shared with him only some of the details of the betrayal and deception that took place and that I didn't want to be anywhere near all that pain nor the people involved. He believed me and I knew he was genuine so I told him more.

Then he validated my character. He only knew me for three weeks and during those weeks I was barely holding it together. I was living in hell, surrounded by a mess of toxic and abusive people in my workplace. Nonetheless, he saw through it all and told me I was the most real thing he experienced there. He was sad to hear what happened and that I had left. He told me that he was going to take a big step back from all those involved. He assured me that he had faith that I was going to find another way to help people and share my love with the world.

I remember reading his text as I was sitting in my parents' garage smoking in my pajamas with unkempt, greasy hair. I started crying, this time not from pain but instead tears of joy. His words reignited my soul pilot light and I went to take a shower.

I started to reignite my passion and redirect my focus to my purpose and that was the beginning of my way forward. To this day we still communicate several times a week. He has become one of my closest friends and I consider him an adoptive dad.

Once you're encouraged by the mentor, your perspective shifts and you reconsider the challenge of the calling. You may find yourself devouring information via books, blogs, articles, YouTube videos, courses and seminars. You might even describe yourself as obsessed, determined to figure it out and understand what happened and why. You are preparing to embark on the next stage of the healing journey with knowledge and practical training, and you're rebuilding your self-confidence in the process.

I started doing ravenous research online, spending hours and hours every day learning everything I could about PTSD/C-PTSD caused by abuse. I was obsessed with learning. I began directing my energy into contributing validation and healing advice to people in online support groups who had gone through similar abusive experiences.

For the first time in my life, people (other than my close friends) were really valuing the information and energy I was sharing. Up until that point when I tried to teach, coach and add online content no one really cared about what I was offering. The shift was that I was now consciously in contact with my wound and starting to believe in myself. I was turning that wound into a sense of purpose. I was committed to the healing process no matter what it took. The more I helped others, the stronger I felt inside and the more meaning I felt in my life. I felt like I was on to something.

The refusal to answer the calling may go on for some time, even after mentors come into your life. You might find yourself pushing them away and choosing to stay in the suffering because it feels easier to focus outside yourself than inside plus the pull of denial still feels so tempting. Or you might find abusive mentors who return you to the abuse cycle for a while longer. I have also taken that path in the past.

Some people stay here indefinitely, focusing on the external truths of narcissistic abuse, who the narcissist is and how s/he works, what s/he did and how it hurt. While there is a definite relief upon learning this truth and information, it is not empowering on its own and will not lead to healing without taking new action to work on yourself. Until you take action, all your knowledge is like mental masturbation.

It is said that knowledge is power but really knowledge is only potential power. Power comes when you put the knowledge into practice with action.

There is one piece of knowledge that changes everything. When you realize that there is something within yourself that allowed the abuse and manipulation to go on, or that there was a familiar pattern repeating in your life attracting those types of people and experiences, you have the first glimpse of self-responsibility.

That shift in perception is what empowers you to realize that you can do something to change things now. You can accept that the abuse wasn't your fault, and now you can also shift your life moving forward by making new choices.

At first this is a cognitive realization. Then at some point the spontaneous visceral understanding hits you and you're ready to take new action based on your new sense of self-responsibility. That new action is the essence of Crossing The First Threshold.

Chapter 5

Crossing The First Threshold

(5) Crossing The First Threshold[1] is your all-in commitment to the self-healing journey.

You cross this threshold when you take 100%
self- responsibility for your life and the reigns
of your destiny back in your hands.

At this point you're starting to feel **Committed**[2] to living your truth and healing your life.

How will you know you've crossed this threshold? There is a tangible difference in the way you'll feel when you've taken back the steering wheel of self-control. It's almost indescribable yet you will know something shifted. That is the feeling of **Self-empowerment**, and this is the key to entering Stage Two.

For me this moment came about a week after my mentor reignited my soul pilot light. I had started creating a new website for my coaching work and for the first time in a long time I felt a sense of hope and passion about what I was working on.

I went to tell my mother about my exciting plans to get my coaching business up and running again and what I was going to offer. She looked up at me sideways from the dining table where she was sitting among piles and piles of catalogs. I'll never forget that scene.

She was rubbing her forehead exasperated, deeply ashamed of me. "What?! I can't believe you're thinking about doing that coaching again. It's never worked before, so why would it work now? Why don't you just go to the mall and get a job!"

In that moment there was a ripple in the space-time matrix. I suddenly saw her for who she is for the first time. I also saw my own responsibility. I realized she is who she is and I can't change that. I realized it was my responsibility now as an adult to stop going to her for support and empathy because she wasn't capable of that.

I recognized that I needed to set new boundaries with what I share with her and how much I let her into my life. That killjoy energy is so dangerous to my projects when they're in their nascent state. It was a constant theme of our relationship whenever I talked about my joy or dreams, alternating with false support in the form of love-bombing, then followed with subtle little digs and comments to make me doubt myself, feel small or not good enough.

I could finally see her separate from me and could no longer blame her for keeping me stuck. I knew I had to get out of that environment ASAP and even though I didn't have any answers yet, I believed in my ability to figure it out. I took the reigns of my destiny back in my hands and made a full commitment to myself and my journey.

This might even be the first time you've ever felt empowered in your life. Before crossing this threshold, you likely felt incredibly helpless and powerless in life or at least one area of your life. As you cross this threshold, a new sense of self-control over your life leads to a growing sense of empowerment and upgraded self-esteem.

When you take 100% self-responsibility for your life,
you start to experience how your attitudes and actions affect the
world around you. You realize you're not a helpless and powerless
victim of life anymore.

This is the point of no return.

At this moment, you're crossing the threshold between the old, familiar world and that which is unknown. Essentially you're setting out to do what you were scared to do but you know you have to do.

*You may not know exactly how yet, but you now
believe in your ability to figure it out.*

At this turning point, you may need to convince a symbolic
guardian of the threshold to let you cross over. This threshold test
can manifest in many ways. Perhaps one of the abusers from your
past shows up as soon as you take the reigns back. They might try
to lure you into giving up your power again, right at the threshold of
this life-changing decision. It could even be a fear that invites you
to self-sabotage just before you cross the threshold. Essentially the
universe is verifying if you really want to pass through.

Generally this comes from contact attempts. This is what's
referred to as *hoovering*, when the abuser tries to suck you back in
by telling you exactly what you want to hear (eliciting a positive and
receptive feeling from you) or provoking a negative reaction from
you and hooking you back into the abuse cycle that way. Or maybe
you even reach out to an abuser in a moment of weakness. Maybe
it's not the recent abuser, but rather someone from the past or even
the original abuser in your life. Sometimes the guardians of the
threshold even come in swarms.

After I jumped ship from my parents' house, I went to
stay with my friend on the West Coast. She had invited
me to spend the winter there and get on my feet again.
Within the first ten days I realized I needed to leave there
a lot sooner.

The first few days were pretty good, mostly catching
up with a friend I hadn't seen in years. Her words were
saying she was happy I was there. Yet at the same time I
felt like she didn't really want me there. It didn't make
sense so I ignored the feeling.

About a week in, she offered me a ride to another city
an hour and a half away where I had planned to spend a
few days with another friend the following week. I told
her thank you for the offer but no worries because I would
work out the ride. She insisted and insisted on helping me
so I agreed.

Then at the last minute the night before, she suddenly acted like it was a really big deal and she wasn't sure if she could give me the ride because it was going to be a huge inconvenience to her schedule. I was scrambling to make arrangements with just hours before I was supposed to be leaving. That was exactly what I was trying to avoid and the reason I just wanted to make my own plans from the beginning.

I ended up asking my soul sister friend, a single mom of a toddler who I was going to stay with, to drive up most of the way to get me. The friend I was currently staying with decided to drive me part of the way with a lot of tension and suspense leading up to that decision. She spent the whole ride acting put out and going on and on about whether there would be traffic on the way back and if it would mess up her whole day, but she really wants the best for me. I couldn't wait to get out of the car.

I spent several days away and in the presence of my soul sister friend who has been there for me more than once when I've left an abusive person. She was problem-solving with me trying to come up with the next step because I knew I couldn't stay long where I was at and I couldn't go back to my parents' house either.

A couple days after I had returned to my narcissistic friend's apartment, she left me for five days with no cooking gas or hot water. According to her, something crazy happened with the gas line while people were working on the next door apartment sharing the same line. She was given a choice by the management to get a reduction in rent for the next eleven days of inconvenience or for them to put the gas back on immediately with no rent reduction. She chose the reduction in rent and headed out of town with her mom.

Before she left, to divert my attention from the gas issue, she went out to buy a carpet cleaning product and sponges because according to her, my dog was dirtying her carpet. I really didn't see a difference in the short time we had been there and I'm pretty meticulous about cleanliness. It wasn't like I could complain about anything since I was staying there for free and she was helping me. Some covert abusers offer to help so they can control you and that gets very confusing. I was just grateful to be sleeping on an air mattress on her floor while trying to get my life together. While she was gone I put 100% of my energy and time into finding a way out.

During that time in a moment of weakness, I emailed my ex in Portland to tell him I was looking for work there and asking him if he knew of any place that my dog and I could stay while I was getting on my feet. I regretted it immediately. He wrote back to say he didn't know of anything and just wanted to know what was going on in my life.

That week I also heard from my attorney in Peru, who had manipulated me emotionally and sexually then left me hanging with a lot of excuses, taking zero self-responsibility regarding his legal contract that my former business partner never paid me accordingly. The attorney emailed me that week to remind me that I owed him $500 in legal fees, sandwiched between a bunch of subtle blame-shifting language about how he did everything he could and it was my responsibility that my business partner was not trustworthy since all the attorney does is write the contract that the partners had agreed upon. I was so angry. I told him how I felt about his utter failure as an attorney and supposed friendship, and that I wasn't going to pay him because my business partner never paid me according to the contract.

I kept applying online for jobs in Portland, looking for any shred of possibility to get on my feet again. I got an interview at a cannabis dispensary and took it as a sign to leave immediately.

Two days later while I was waiting for my ride to the

airport, my former narcissist friend said that when she was moving away from home her mom said to her, "It's tough to survive out there," as she touched my left elbow. I knew her mom was a narcissistic manipulator. I'd only met her for about thirty seconds, twice, on the landing to her apartment where I was told to wait outside for my friend as if I were a dog. I recognized this phrase as some sort of incantation inviting me to give up and doubt my ability to get on my feet again, so I brushed off her energy with my hand and said, "thank you for everything." I knew that would be the last time I talked to her. Six months later out of the blue she texted me, "I love you." I didn't respond and instead I blocked her.

As I boarded the plane to Portland the captain announced that there had been "unsettling winds" up and down the West Coast and we might have a bumpy ride. How very symbolic.

Days after I arrived in Portland, I received the last email from my ex. He didn't know I was back in town, though sometimes the timing of these abusers is uncanny. He was simply putting out the feelers to see what I was up to. Abusers rarely want to know *how* you are, they just want to know *what* you're doing. I finally chose not to answer. And that was the end of that.

I started setting new contact boundaries with my parents too because I was realizing how hard it was to focus on building my new life with my mom's couched words of abuse disguised as concern in my ear. They had helped me to get on my feet too but I knew I had to break free from that financial help ASAP otherwise I would always feel guilted into having the frequency of contact they wanted. I finally understood that even phone contact with my mom was dangerous. She would say the littlest things that really sounded like concern on the surface yet somehow she could take the wind right out of my sails like no other person on this planet.

I knew I could no longer invest my energy in any negative thoughts like the fears and doubts that she loves to plant. My own mind would then continue to run that program even when she wasn't in my ear. I had internalized her negativity reality paradigm. I knew all of that had to go if I wanted to have any chance at succeeding. So I went all in. I became a mental ninja allowing only positive thoughts to take seed in my mind, dismissing the fears and doubts. I was owning that responsibility fiercely, all day long, stalking my self-talk.

I finally had the realization that in order to create the life I wanted to live, I could only allow that reality in my mind. I stopped sharing anything with my mother that wasn't in the past tense. Finally understanding just how dangerous her energy is to anything that I'm creating, I fiercely protected my plans and dreams for the first time in my life. I felt guilty not telling her everything as I had been trained to do, but I knew it was the only way forward and out of the gravity of the black hole.

Statistics say abuse survivors go back an average of seven times. Don't be surprised if you do another round or several before finally crossing the First Threshold. Most of us do. I certainly went back for my share of frying-pan-to-the-head lessons over the years. Before I understood what was happening, instead of moving forward in the healing journey, I kept getting re-victimized by new and old abusers.

Right before this threshold, you're sick and tired of feeling exhausted, worthless, powerless, and helpless.

You don't want to feel powerless one more day,
so you take the leap of faith
and commit to the journey no matter what it takes.

Crossing the First Threshold is the empowerment of taking 100% self-responsibility for your life and the choices you make, now and moving forward. You stop looking for a rescuer and you decide to play the protagonist role in your own rescue.

You can feel this inner shift as you take self-control of your life back. Almost instantly you'll notice how much more energy you have now that it's not being drained through feeling victimized. You'll likely notice a sudden reduction in your sense of helplessness and powerlessness in life as you move past this threshold into Stage Two.

STAGE TWO

Survivor Stage
Empowered
Radical Self-care

Chapter 6

Summary of Stage Two

As you enter Stage Two you'll start to discover who your allies are. You'll also discover who your enemies are and you'll be tested in the process. You will be tested over and over in relationships and challenging life experiences. These tests are not easy but with each one that you pass, you gain greater strength and momentum forward. With each one that you fail, you have the opportunity to learn something new and grow.

This is the stage where you dedicate yourself
to radical self-care.

In Stage Two you'll feel a need to tell your story in great detail, to yourself and others, and you'll begin to dig into the past as well as exploring more deeply the present feelings that are still with you from your past experiences of abuse.

During this stage it might seem like you are getting worse, but
actually what's happening is a surfacing, uncovering and revealing
of everything that was stuffed away so you could survive the
abusive relationship or environment.
Once you are in a safe refuge, it all starts coming out.

These feelings might come out as psychosomatic symptoms like rashes, pain, illnesses, injuries, etc. They might come out as intense emotional ups and downs. Just when you think you've hit a moment of peace, something new will come up to be resolved. There might be moments when you're thinking, *can I get a friggin' break?*

During Stage Two, triggers will frequently evoke a deja vu sensation in your subconscious and you'll face more and more of the past as if you were reliving it. Often you have no choice but deal with what's showing up because you can't focus on anything else.

*At the second threshold, the turning point of Stage Two, you're
going to face your deepest fears and that which holds the greatest
power over your life.
This is the moment the trauma bond breaks
and the shame dies with it.*

This is also the mourning stage. There's a lot of death and loss to mourn along the way... the loss of a connection that meant a lot to you, a love you lost, as well as (in many cases) the safe and nurturing childhood you didn't have and the loving mother and/or father you never had (if you grew up with a narcissistic parent or two), plus the death of your old false sense of self. It may seem overwhelming and never-ending when you're looking at all the processing and mourning that there is to do, but it gets better and better along the way as you move through it.

Marking the shift between Stage Two and Three, is an opportunity that gives you something new to fight for. At this threshold you are forced to see a person or relationship in your life, now without the goggles of the trauma bond. You'll have a dilemma to choose between your growth/healing or the toxic relationship/situation that you thought you wanted.

*Standing at the third threshold at the end of Stage Two,
you confirm the transformation that you have been working on by
making a decision to protect your
peace and choose a new reality.*

Stage Two is the longest stage of the self-healing journey. Often survivors stay here indefinitely before actualizing themselves into the Thriver Stage. Some people never leave this stage, getting stuck before the Second Threshold and revisiting the past over and over or staying in limbo and opting out of further growth. It's certainly better than being stuck in the Victim Stage. However, I encourage you to keep going. There's so much more amazingness to experience in Stage Three and it's worth the work and dedication that it takes to get there.

Chapter 7

The Common Markers of Stage Two

- insomnia and restless sleep, nightmares at times, waking multiple times a night and difficulty falling back asleep

- frequent triggering and flashbacks evoking unresolved and painful memories and emotions from the past

- dissociation (you may still be dissociating during this stage but not as much as Stage One)

- rumination about the past and abusers (looking for deeper "why" answers)

- shame and false guilt, more intense when the memories and flashbacks are taking place

- bargaining (this is when you are trying to believe that maybe the abuser didn't mean to hurt you, and maybe if a certain event hadn't happened then everything would be alright)

- you'll have periods of avoidance and trying to go back to "normal" or even convincing yourself that you're doing better than you are (this is hard work so naturally you'll want to not deal with it at times)

- challenging emotions first increase (through the triggers and flashbacks/memories) then decrease later in Stage Two (as you feel them and process them)

- alternation between anger and depression

- fantasies of revenge and justice

- in and out of denial until you cross the Second Threshold later in Stage Two (where the trauma bond breaks)

- resistance to facing the truth at times and preferring to live in the fantasy that you want to see

- resentment about having to do the self-healing work because it's so unfair

- wishing it would all just go away by telling the story (talking about it is an important step but it's not going to heal it for you)

- desperation to speed up process

- thinking you're more healed than you are (until the next trigger happens and you realize you've got more work to do)

- hyper-vigilance of words, actions, facial expressions and feelings of others

- often misinterpreting others' intentions and fearing attack, deceit and betrayal

- unsure who to trust (either too trusting of everyone or unable to trust anyone)

- cynical about people in general, or towards a certain gender, race or other common characteristic of the abuser

- panic attacks and anxiety (reduced from Stage One but still present)

- occasional wishing for a rescuer (though not to the extent of Stage One)

- still somewhat isolated and disconnected from your ordinary world and social life

- many failures along the way, ups and downs as you learn and grow (Les Brown said, "You will fail your way to success," and that totally applies here)

- a growing sense of momentum and strength as you progress along the way

- feeling more successful and accomplished in most areas of your life

- taking greater control of your inner world and how you respond to life

- defensiveness (you may find yourself extra defensive about what happened to you and your present state especially when people don't get it)

- fear of being victimized again (you'll be extra sensitive to perceived deception and betrayal)

- functioning in most areas of your life (you're really starting to get your life back in this stage yet occasionally you'll need hours or days to just zone out and take a break)

- seeing the patterns much more clearly of the recent abuse as well as the connection to childhood abuse or neglect that may likely have taken place

- processing the childhood wounds that were similar to the abuse in adulthood

- an increasing, healthy sense of self-responsibility while releasing the old programming of taking on the responsibility of the abuser's issues

- healthier boundaries and an improved ability to say NO

- restoring a sense of self-validation and approval instead of people-pleasing and seeking approval from others

- better balance of selfish and selfless (both are important and now you're learning how to put your own needs first more often in order to be in better balance)

- greater self-compassion and self-acceptance

- more in touch with your feelings and meeting your needs (sometimes you still might ignore your feelings or needs and then end up breaking down in order to deal with what's coming up)

- Inner Child is terrified at first and then eventually becomes more integrated the more s/he feels safe and taken care of

- every time you fall down you'll get back up quicker and more easily

- seeing new possibilities and new potential in yourself and life

- less suffering and pain as you process the memories and feelings of the past

- occasional confusion and lack of clarity but not like Stage One where it was almost constant

strength when it feels like you're getting tested constantly and struggling to swim your way through it. This recovery process is messy. Trust in your process and be willing to get messy. These transformational experiences are making you stronger.

Identifying Your Inner Strengths

A really helpful practice during this stage is to look at the inner strengths that you relied on to survive the abuse i.e. your intuition and self-trust, which maybe you listened to in exactly the moment that you needed to in order to save yourself. For example, maybe you somehow just knew that the only way out was to sneak away quietly, then later you read online that the only way to leave a psychopath is to sneak away. Or maybe you sensed you just had to block that person to protect your health, sanity and wellbeing even before you read about No Contact.

Reflect back upon the ways that you knew how to do something without anyone telling you. What internal resources did you rely upon to set boundaries, to take action to get out and to survive?

This will help you to rely on your inner strength, knowing that anytime you feel something is off with anyone new, you can and will leave the person immediately because you can trust yourself to recognize it and act upon it. This will also help you to remember which internal strengths you can call upon now to get through the daily tests of this stage.

Self-control & Self-responsibility

There are some things in this self-healing journey that you can control, and some that you cannot. Recognizing this difference will save you a lot of frustration and exasperation.

Self-control is the only real control there is in this life.
You can control how you show up in every moment.
You cannot control anything outside of you.

Letting go of trying to control what is outside of you requires a growing sense of self-trust and acceptance that life happens and most of that is out of your control, while also knowing that if something happens you're going to be able to figure it out and get through it.

The more you own your self-responsibility, the more you recognize that the one thing you can control is how you show up... and that's a lot of power. A growing sense of self-control is a powerful healing indicator during this stage as you are leaving behind the learned helplessness of the past.

A huge piece of the self-control that you're building in Stage Two is responding versus reacting. You'll notice that the more you're able to control your emotional reactions to people and life and instead respond from a place of authenticity and empowerment, the better you feel and the more progress you make because you actually have the energy to focus on what you want to whereas before you were expending so much energy reacting to every emotional provocation and manipulation that comes from the outside.

Something magical happens when you change yourself. The universe changes how it responds to you and so you start to meet different people and situations than the past.

Triggers & Emotional Balancing

Emotional balancing is an important part of Stage Two. All kinds of emotions will be coming up during this stage and at times you may feel overwhelmed. You'll reach moments of relative calmness and then another storm will surge again as a memory comes up or a trigger reminds you of the past. You might feel rage, anger, resentment, sadness, grief and nostalgia among many other feelings that you'll need to feel, process and resolve so you can move beyond them. There are a lot of ups and downs. You'll find that you have longer periods of emotional calm as you progress with your healing. At first it might be an hour, then a few hours, then half a day, then a whole day, then days at a time before the next emotional down comes. You will know you're growing emotional resilience when you bounce back quicker and easier each time you're down. Even though the emotional response might be uncomfortable, triggers are not all negative. Triggers are caused when something reminds your subconscious of a painful, traumatic experience in the past so you can face it and release it. It's not a rational understanding kind of thing.

Have you ever been brushing your teeth in the morning and suddenly you have a flashback of your dreams the night before? It's logically unrelated to brushing your teeth but something subconscious triggered that memory. The conscious, rational, intellectual understanding part of the brain is not the domain of trauma, which is why talking about it alone does not heal it.

Trauma is managed by the emotional and primal areas of the brain, which correspond to the subconscious mind.
We have to go beyond intellectual understanding to heal the trauma.

It can be scary when we don't understand what's happening. To move through this stage with greater ease, start recognizing when you're getting triggered and notice what's triggering you. I highly recommend writing this down so you can see the patterns over time. This helps you reverse-engineer and unwind your trauma patterns so you can clear them and it will help you make the subconscious, conscious. When you recognize that you're getting triggered, remind yourself that this is for a reason so you can face something that has been repressed below the level of your awareness and now you can clear it. This avoids the downward spiraling crashes that triggers can bring on when we aren't moving through them with the light of consciousness as a guide.

Anger processing is really important during this stage. Your abuser might have tried to blame you for your anger about the abuse. Most of them do. They like to focus on your reaction to the abuse and not the abuse itself.

It's normal and natural for you to be angry about the abuse that happened to you. That's called righteous anger and it's different

than the toxic form of anger
that an abuser uses to control and intimidate others.

The anger you feel is the result of someone violating you. It's okay to feel angry about that. The anger motivates you to do something about it. However, you don't want to keep that anger inside your body for too long or it will start to eat you alive. It can become inflammation, muscle tension, pain, headaches and even cancer. For some people the repressed anger turns inward into depression.

The anger needs to come out through a form of authentic self-expression, when you're in the safety of your privacy. It's really powerful to use your voice to emote the anger because it's empowering and transforms it into a sense of strength after the silence you've carried for months or years. You can also choose to beat a pillow or mattress, or even a boxing bag. Some people may prefer to put on heavy metal music and dance intensely, releasing the anger through the body thrashing around. Be careful not to hurt yourself, of course. You'll find an Anger Processing exercise in the digital courses on my website if you want more help with that process.

Once the anger starts to clear, what you'll find is the more vulnerable emotions like sadness, despair, shame and grief start to come out because the anger is the protective emotional guard. Allow yourself to cry and release these when the vulnerable emotions come up. Sometimes you might feel like you're crying for no reason. There's a reason, it's just not conscious yet. You may find that when you provide a safe container for yourself to release the tears that you get spontaneous insights and revelations about why it's coming up. It's really helpful to write those down right away because they're coming from deep in your subconscious and you might forget them because they haven't been integrated into your conscious mind yet.

Reparenting the Inner Child

Stage Two is where the reparenting of the Inner Child takes place.

Facing the childhood wound is key to moving through this stage.

This is usually where the pattern of abuse or neglect began, or at the very least the painful feeling of loneliness, rejection or not being heard and/or seen that set you up for an abusive relationship as an adult. It's an imprint that you received through some sort of programming as a child.

Adult abusive relationships feel familiar when you've been used to feeling a certain way most of your life, and that's often why people overlook the initial red flags and intuitive feelings that something is off. When the adult abuser reminds you of how you felt growing up, you might associate that abusive behavior with love and then normalize it by saying, "that's just how so-and-so is" which you might have heard in your own family. Your own neurons will betray your conscious mind in this process. No matter how much you know and understand about abuse, until you resolve the underlying wound and take a firm stance against tolerance for abuse, your subconscious will keep magnetizing more experiences that remind you of how you already feel.

This is what leads to the repetition compulsion of experiencing the same hurt over and over with different faces in a subconscious attempt to resolve it.

It's important to look into your childhood wound so you can see how this pattern has been following you in some way or another all your life. It's also important to work on rebuilding your Inner Child's trust in you, as the Inner Parent, giving her/him the unconditional love and validation that s/he never had. You can do this by checking in with your feelings multiple times a day, recognizing what you need and then meeting that need for yourself. This simple but powerful exercise helps rebuild your Inner Child's trust in that his/her needs are going to be met and it's safe to express feelings. Check out John Bradshaw's work on this topic, in particular his book *Homecoming*.[1] You might also want to check out my Inner Child Integration guided visualization available on my website.

Reprogramming the Self-talk

Reprogramming the self-talk is one of the most important parts of the work during Stage Two and one of the most powerful techniques that will transform your life when you do it consistently over time.

Become like a ninja stalking your thoughts.

Identify the negative thoughts that have to go so you can experience a more positive mindset and better quality of life. Start reprogramming the negative, fearful thoughts with positive ones. All day long observe your Inner Dialogue so you can notice these thoughts and reprogram them.

Your self-talk is a constant reminder of your belief systems. This is where your perspective comes from.

If you grew up in a narcissistic household, you were programmed into a negativity paradigm of fear and doubt. You can experience this in adult relationships too. In order to liberate yourself to create the life you actually want to live, you need to rewrite those scripts in your self-talk.

Your perspective, how you look at yourself and the world,
is what determines your reality.

Nothing will really shift in your life until you start to master this domain. When you first start looking at your self-talk you'll notice just how negative it is. You probably received a lot of negative, doubtful and fearful messages as a child if you grew up with a narcissistic parent and then again as an adult in the abusive relationship/s. Be willing to dedicate yourself to rewriting this overwhelming negativity script every time you see a negative thought go by. When you do this consistently all day long, you'll notice by the end of the first month how much less negativity there is and how much clearer your mind is.

The reprogramming process is essentially training your "inner critic" to become a helpful ally instead of a master saboteur. I highly recommend my Reprogramming Flashbacks & Self-Talk exercise available as a digital download on my website to help you master this practice. This topic of reprogramming the self-talk also comes up as an important part of my Self-Care Mastery Course.

Next Level Boundaries

Here in Stage Two, you're working on next-level boundaries. By now, you've gotten most of the toxic people out of your life and you'll likely notice now that there are still a few stragglers left who have to go in order to protect your peace.

One really important next level boundary that you'll be working on during Stage Two is saying NO. In Stage One you started to put this into practice. Now in Stage Two, there is a noticeable shift from your past orientation of people-pleasing (self-abandonment) into radical self-care (self-love) as you are consistently prioritizing your needs more without feeling as guilty in the process. This is such a liberating shift in how you interact with the world.

You're worrying less about people-pleasing because you are starting to value your wellbeing more than what others think.

Canadian physician, Dr. Gabor Maté says that people-pleasing will kill you. He did a great video on YouTube called *When The Body Says No*[2] based on his book with the same title. In the video he reads obituaries of people who died by people-pleasing. It's eye-opening and sobering for those of us who recognize this tendency to put other's needs before our own.

When you start actively prioritizing your needs after you've spent a lifetime putting others first, initially this feels foreign and often comes with a heavy sense of false guilt but little by little it will feel more comfortable and you'll notice how drastically your life changes for the better in this process. Mastering the ability to say NO is not only a key part of letting go of your people-pleasing tendencies, but also conserving your energy so you can invest it in healing and building your dreams moving forward.

At the Growth Summit in 2016[3], Dean Graziosi said, "Successful people say no 80% of the time." When I heard that I realized why I hadn't been successful. I was putting aside my own needs and priorities in order to take care of other people's needs and false emergencies. Nowadays I'm very clear with myself what is a yes and what is a no. High performance expert, Brendon Burchard[4] says, "What is helpful to people is you living your truth, you serving your highest good in this world and not everybody's speedy needy requests."

By now you're also getting more confident and comfortable enforcing your boundaries when toxic people react negatively to them. Toxic people hate boundaries because these mean they can't get what they want. They will usually take this out on you and try to violate your boundary either directly (through overt aggression with words or actions) or indirectly (through guilt-tripping or shaming you for having those boundaries). These are excellent opportunities to remind yourself that you're not here to please others.

Your #1 responsibility is you.

If you're a hardcore people-pleaser, you may want to write a mantra like, *I am my #1 responsibility* on a post-it note and put it around your house where you can see it over and over until it sinks in.

If you're meeting new people, you might notice some of them are toxic. These encounters are opportunities to put your next level boundaries into practice.

During Stage Two, you're now fine-tuning your boundaries with a constant, daily inventory of the people that you're allowing into your life and most especially, who you're allowing into your Inner Circle.

Redefining Your Inner Circle

Notice who are the five or six people you spend the most time and energy with. This could be in person, on the phone or even online. You become like the people you most surround yourself with so choose carefully. Write down their names and why you like hanging out with them, what characteristics they have that you admire and what impact they have on your life.

If you realize their impact is not positive and you don't want to become like them, then move those people out to the periphery (or cut them out entirely) in order to responsibly own the space, time and energy that you give to those who are closest to you.

Choosing your Inner Circle consciously is very important to protect your sense of peace and joy.

The most dangerous part about being in contact with toxic people is the temptation to subscribe to their reality. It's important to maintain your self-awareness and recognize when someone else is trying to obligate you to adopt their perspective, which you know is not resonant with your truth. In those cases I like to remind myself of the mantra, *that's not my reality!*

As you do the inventory of your Inner Circle, ask yourself if the people you hang out with are toxic and draining to your physical, psychological and spiritual wellbeing or if they're supportive and nurturing. How do you know the difference? Notice how you feel when you think about them. Notice how you feel when you're with them and then afterward. Give them a particular text tone on your phone and notice how you feel when you hear that sound. It could be really helpful to journal those feelings so you can track them over time.

Be careful that you're not accepting toxic, draining people in your life simply because you're afraid to be alone. It's much better to be alone for a period of healing so you can focus your energy on taking care of you and healing from the past, than it is to keep feeding people who are sucking the energy out of you, leaving you with nothing to invest in your recovery. Toxic people will keep you stuck in the negative feedback loop. The sooner you get them out, the better.

Enlist more allies during this stage so you can stand in your truth and speak the unspeakable with witnesses who validate your feelings and encourage you in your healing. It's so hard to speak

93

about the abuse because of the imposed code of silence, the deep shame and irrational loyalty to the abusers caused by the trauma bond, as well as the terror of them finding out that you told the truth. When you have supportive people in your Inner Circle, it's a lot easier to find the bravery to speak your truth.

Upgrading Your Relationships

The first relationship that you work to heal during Stage Two is the relationship you have with yourself.

Astrologer and soul coach, Christopher Witecki[5] coined the term "ME-rriage" to describe the importance of the relationship you have with yourself. All of your self-care (and growing self-love) starts there.

As you restore your relationship with yourself through the practice of radical self-care, you begin to apply that outward toward your relationships with others and the universe. When you're taking good care of yourself, your subconscious feels how much you respect yourself. When you meet someone who is not respecting you, it's now so obvious.

When you are disappointed or unhappy with people and the world around you, look inside yourself first to see what you can change. Maybe you realize you can change the way you're responding to that person or situation. Maybe you need to reduce how much you share with that person. Or maybe you realize you've got to get yourself out of a certain situation in order to feel good.

Honor yourself in order to know which relationships in your life are honorable.

Rebuilding Self-trust

During Stage Two you're going to be rebuilding your self-trust through the Inner Child reparenting as well as listening to your intuition more and acting on it. The more you listen to your intuition and take action accordingly, the quicker your self-trust will grow.

It's really helpful while you're reviewing the past, to look back and recognize how your intuition knew that something wasn't right with the abuser from the beginning. Notice all the little signs and the ways your intuition tried to show you. It can be helpful to take notes. The point of this reflection is not to beat yourself up about not listening to your intuition, but rather to rebuild your sense of self-trust by realizing that your intuition works just fine and to empower yourself by noticing how you could take action according to your intuition the next time you feel something similar.

Notice how your intuition sends you messages so you can pay more attention to them. Does it come visually in the form of images? Or is it auditory, where you hear words a person said or other meaningful sounds? Or does your intuition send you messages in the form of an inner knowing or feeling that you can't really explain?

Notice how your intuition also speaks through your body. One of the most common bodily intuition sensations I hear from clients when they knew something wasn't right in the relationship, was a strange feeling in the stomach or an icky sensation.

Once you notice how your intuition sends you the message that something isn't okay, now you know how to recognize it when it shows up again.

It's really helpful to journal this stuff because you might have powerful insights and revelations in one moment of clarity and forget it the next. It's also helpful to keep adding to your healing journal as more intuitive feelings come up. It will be so validating for you down the road.

Stepping into Integrity

It's also important to rebuild your sense of integrity by identifying your values and what's important to you, then acting in alignment with those. When your actions are out of alignment with your core values you're going to feel awful about yourself because essentially you're not respecting yourself. My 12-Week SANA Series contains an episode on defining and aligning your values and vision. The exercises in there will help you get into integrity with yourself.

The key to rebuilding self-respect is to work on your integrity.

You'll likely find yourself starting to question the meaning in the traumatic events of the past during this stage. It can be helpful to reverse-engineer what happened, how the abuse/manipulation took place, what they did and how they conned/deceived you. This practice is not intended to beat yourself up for not seeing it or for staying beyond the point where you saw it for what it was, but rather to fully, consciously recognize how it happened so you know how to identify the signs immediately if this pattern ever shows up again.

Notice the moment/s when you sacrificed your integrity in order to stay in connection with the abuser. This is really key to moving forward with a growing sense of self-trust. If someone betrays you, ask yourself how you betrayed yourself. Chances are you had a feeling, maybe you didn't like someone or something felt wrong, but you normalized, rationalized, or minimized it and went on. That was the moment of self-betrayal.

The abuse is never your fault, however your responsibility now is to honor your integrity so you don't risk the self-betrayal happening again.

Every time I've been betrayed I can recognize where that self-betrayal took place first. If I had been faithful to myself and my integrity in those situations, I would have set a boundary and/or walked away instead of keep engaging.

The dirty trick of the abusers is to invite you to step out of your integrity using your own free will. That causes regret when you know you didn't show up as the best version of yourself and it gives the abuser a weapon to use against you by constantly reminding you of your shortcomings. That is what forms the vicious circle of shame and self-blame. Self-acceptance is a lot easier when you know you're in integrity with yourself.

Often it's when we step out of our own integrity that's the hardest part to forgive. Again, this reflection on self-betrayal is not to beat yourself up about it, but rather to notice where your own choice to ignore your intuition and step out of your integrity led you down a road you didn't want to go. This way, when another temptation shows up inviting you out of integrity, you'll know that you want to choose your integrity first over pleasing another person, no matter what excuse or rationalization they have and no matter how much you want them to like you.

Developing Presence & Authenticity
to Overcome the Loneliness

During Stage Two it's important to develop a greater sense of presence (being fully in the here and now) and authenticity (being/ expressing your true self). As you cultivate more presence and authenticity you will notice how the loneliness starts to diminish.

It seems so simple and cliche but dedicating yourself to being present and authentic when you're alone and with others is a very powerful practice that will change your life.

It's often the simple things that make the biggest difference when practiced consistently over time.

Nowadays most people aren't present at all. There are infinite distractions in our world, most notably digital devices but also the internal bombardment of thoughts caused by living a life without focus and discipline.

Being present with another person is one of the most beautiful gifts you can offer them and that will change the quality of your relationships drastically.

Being present with yourself will change your life. It will help you notice your feelings and needs as well as your perceptions of yourself, other people and situations. When you are present and not distracted or dissociated, you will notice when something is off. When you are present you will be able to know what you need to do in the moment to protect and honor yourself. When you are present you have so much more energy to invest in transforming yourself and your life. Your presence puts you back into a state of connection with the world around you and the loneliness dissolves.

When you are standing in your authenticity, you feel good about yourself. When you are allowing yourself to be your true self, you feel confident and proud of who you are. You are able to accomplish things and feel a sense of competency. You have the clarity and decisiveness about what you want and who you are. When you're not in your authenticity you will feel low self-worth because you're pretending to be something you're not. Essentially inauthenticity is the foundation of a false sense self. You may have developed that false self to people-please others in order to receive validation and approval. This causes depression because deep down you know this is not your authentic self.

When you're present and showing up as your authentic self around others you'll notice pretty quickly who does not belong in your life.

Abusers won't appreciate your authenticity and they'll want you to be different to please them. They might express this through jokes by subtly putting you down or outright making fun of you and then they'll tell you, "it's just a joke" or "you're so serious/sensitive." Walk away from those people. They don't respect you and they will only tempt you to compromise your authenticity and possibly even question your sanity.

Unleashing Your Authentic Self-expression

During Stage Two it's important to find new ways of expressing yourself and your creativity. Your authentic self-expression was probably quite hindered from the abuse (and maybe even stifled since childhood), so it might feel foreign at first to let your heart, mind and body freely express yourself. Maybe you were criticized a lot and maybe you even experienced a lot of cruelty from abusers, causing you to shut down and only let a small part of yourself out for fear of rejection.

Self-expression is about letting yourself shine
in your authenticity.
It's about unapologetically being your true self.

If you're standing in your authenticity and integrity and other people don't like it, step away from those relationships because they will only tempt you into dimming your light and hiding your true self. When you dim your true self you are doing the world a disservice. The world needs you to be yourself and carry out your unique life purpose and mission that you were born for. If you've been through such an awful experience as abuse, I can guarantee that you are here to do something meaningful by shining your light for others. What you choose to do with that light is up to you. Let your authenticity guide you. Do not stop for the haters. They're just there to remind you that you're doing something meaningful, which threatens their ability to have power and control over you or others.

When you are authentically expressing yourself
the universe supports you because you're living in your truth.

Speaking Your Truth

It's not going to heal you simply by speaking your story, however speaking it is the start of taking the power away from the abuser and returning it to you. Relentlessly facing the truth is a big part of dissolving the Cognitive Dissonance and piercing the denial.

Speaking your truth starts to relieve you from the burden of the
shame caused by the abuse and this is
what weakens the trauma bond.

Speaking your truth is not a betrayal or gossip. It's about telling your story and it's imperative to the healing process. *If the people who abused you wanted you to speak kindly of them, then they should have treated you better.*

The consequences of other people's behavior
is not your responsibility.

Portia diRossi wrote in her book *Lightness of Being*[6], "We are only as sick as our secrets." Sometimes we even keep secrets from ourselves, especially during abuse, due to the deep sense of shame that was programmed into us.

During this stage, you may be mostly alone for a while in terms of your social life, especially if like most of us you realized that the majority of people in your life were toxic. Maybe you're fortunate to have some supportive friends and family, and if so that's wonderful. You may choose to seek out more therapy and/or holistic healing modalities as you feel called to, to help you connect with your truth and manage the psychosomatic symptoms as well as the pain of everything you're sifting through from the past. Be sure to surround yourself only with people who support you speaking your truth. Those who are threatened by you speaking your truth will only try to sabotage your recovery by planting doubts and fear in your mind or invalidating your truth. Stay away from them to honor your truth.

As you start owning your truth more and getting the wrong people out of your life, you'll be creating more healthy, supportive relationships that resonate with your truth and encourage you to grow and shine. It becomes a positive feedback loop.

Reclaiming the Places

At a certain point during Stage Two, you'll want to start reclaiming the places and things that you gave up in order to not feel the pain of the past. This is referred to as prolonged exposure, where you start revisiting your fears little by little. There may be particular places you have been avoiding during the earlier healing stages so you don't have to run into your ex or be confronted with the painful memories that took place there. You might have been so hurt in your relationship that you haven't dated anyone else in a long time, and it is really helpful in the early stages of healing to take a break from dating. At some point when you feel ready, and often when the universe calls you out of your comfort zone, you can choose to return to the places and activities that you have been avoiding during the more vulnerable stages of the recovery.

When you take it slowly and gradually, you'll start desensitizing yourself to the triggers and fear so you can gain more confidence and strength to reclaim your life.

You'll realize that what you once feared so much, no longer has power over you.

The key is to not overwhelm yourself in the process by taking on too much or going too fast. You'll need to find that balance for yourself. I find it's really helpful when reclaiming these places, to focus on the feeling of gratitude that you survived and grew, reminding yourself this is now and not the past, that you're safe, that you took your power back and left, then started to transform your life. Notice how different your life is now compared to then and feel that gratitude.

This practice of reclaiming the places is clearing the energetic grid so you can create new memories and positive associations with places and activities.

Taking New Risks

In Stage One and early Stage Two it's necessary to take time out for your healing and strengthening, but once you near the end of Stage Two, in order to keep growing you're going to need to challenge yourself, which will involve taking more risk.

One of the interesting things about life and recovery is the less you risk yourself, the less you learn and grow. I don't mean to be reckless and throwing responsibility to the wind. There's a necessary balance. You'll need to take some risks if you want to heal and accomplish anything in life.

If you allow the trauma and fears from the past to cause you to take less risks in life, like if you isolate yourself for a long period of time beyond the initial stages of recovery, you may find that you don't even try to connect with others in social interactions any more because it feels safer alone at home. This can go on for years and years and can keep a person in a state of depression. Or maybe you have a growing sense of purpose in your heart and you want to create an online or local business or support group to help others, but if you don't allow yourself to risk failure and face your fears, then you might never contribute your gift to the world.

Taking risks for growth is about doing something new, something challenging, and sharing more of you with others while maintaining healthy boundaries in the process and not worrying about pleasing others.

We all make mistakes and there will be some failures along the way, but those are all part of the learning experience into growth. As long as you learn something, then you transmute the failure into an opportunity for growth. If you don't ever put yourself out there again you'll miss out on all the experiences and learning opportunities that are available for you to grow as well as thrive in life.

Celebrate Your Successes

Celebrate your successes along the way too, even the little victories. Remind yourself of your points of progress due to the effort that you have been investing in your self-care. This is so important for building confidence and momentum forward. Plus the celebration makes the Inner Child really joyful and that unleashes more of your authenticity and creativity.

The Jump from Stage Two to Stage Three

There are two thresholds in this stage. These turning points are explained in more detail in the following Rite of Passage chapters. The first one is the turning point in your character transformation. It's where the spontaneous breaking of the trauma bond takes place by facing your biggest fear, that which holds the greatest power over your life. As you cross the Second Threshold you'll notice a dramatic reduction in your sense of fear and anxiety and instead a growing sense of peace. You'll also notice the shame dies and in its place a new sense of self-acceptance starts to grow. This threshold can feel like you're entering Stage Three already, however there is still another test on the horizon before you can shift into thriving.

The next turning point, the Third Threshold marks the shift into Stage Three, where you face a dilemma and make a noble choice between what you think you want and what you actually need, restoring your self-trust and confirming the transformation that you made during Stage Two. In the decision-making process, you release the tension caused by your ego attachments to what you thought you wanted and you'll notice that you feel much more energized. At this point you are now owning your reality and you know you got this!

Chapter 9

The Rite of Passage: Stage Two
Transformation

During Stage Two, you'll start experimenting with new conditions such as your new sense of self-responsibility and empowerment. This stage is predominantly internally focused as you learn how to see yourself and the world in new ways.

The self-empowerment that you embraced at the First Threshold has now launched you into a new way of interacting with the world. Stage Two feels like unfamiliar territory at first. You're now well out of your comfort zone and while that's scary, it's also exciting. You and your life will be changing a lot.

The ease with which you flow though this stage depends largely on how you are dealing internally with the changes in your life as well as your consistency and dedication to the work that you are doing to transform yourself.

During this stage you may feel like you're in a supernatural world. There may be moments when you feel a sense of timelessness. You'll be revisiting the past a lot and still having flashbacks affecting the present moment. What you'll find is that the particular flashbacks that come up are somehow related to the themes that you're working on in the present moment in your life. It's all connected and you'll be weaving together the patterns and storyline of your life. It can sometimes feel like you're living in the past even though you know you're in the present, because the feelings about the past can be so intense, vivid and real.

Stage Two starts off with **(6) Tests, Allies, and Enemies**[1] revealing themselves. They can turn up right before and also after the First Threshold. You'll be **Disoriented**[2] at first by the many challenges offering you opportunities to learn and grow. You'll discover plenty of obstacles on the healing path. These can come in the form of interpersonal relationships or events of *force majeure*.

Sometimes those who you think are your Allies, turn out to be Enemies and Tests.

Your character and your commitment to your self-empowerment will be tested frequently during this stage of healing as you are **Weathering the Storm**. You'll have the opportunity to develop a new way of responding to people and life instead of the old ways of reacting to everything. It may seem like everything is testing you during this stage.

The obstacles will try to thwart your progress.
Use that as motivation to keep moving forward.
Keep going and never, ever give up.

It takes even longer to get through this stage if you don't have someone to learn from, some people who figured some things out and can show you what they did that worked as well as the mistakes they made so you can avoid the pitfalls and take a shorter path. This is where your Allies come in.

The more you learn from your Allies the faster you'll move through this stage.

I know, you can't just manifest these people at will and sometimes this path can feel oh so lonely when it seems like no one is showing up or when the ones who do show up are toxic people. If you find yourself incredibly alone, keep working at your self-care and personal development, and stay out of the rescue fantasies. Don't let go of the reigns now that you've taken them back in your hands at the First Threshold.

Rescue fantasies often lead to attracting abusive people masquerading as rescuers and helpers. Remember you are responsible for your life.

Sometimes miracles take place. You might notice at times that as soon as you wish to manifest a person to teach you something, and you are 100% committed to take the action necessary to implement it, suddenly that someone appears in your life. Trust that they will show up when you're ready. This universe is magical that way. You will find exactly the message you need right when you need it from the person who can best deliver it to you in your surroundings, if you're open to receiving it. This happens time and time again in my life, evoking powerful feelings of gratitude and awe.

Some Allies might show up multiple times in your life when you need their message and inspirational presence.

While I was staying with the narcissistic friend at the beach and trying to figure out what to do, I spent several days down in San Diego with one of my soul sisters. She had recently found a wonderful man who loves her and her son, and she was making big strides forward in her holistic career. Her fiery presence always encourages me to empower myself and not to be anyone's victim.

I hadn't seen her in several years since I'd escaped a psychopath in LA when she took me in for a month before moving to the East Coast. I would not have regained my sanity and inner strength without her being around me that month. During the years in between, she and I had both moved to new places and come back to California.

She was currently living in a house with other single mothers and their kids so she couldn't offer me a place to stay as she had in the past. That worked out for the best because I needed to figure it out for myself and this time the only way I was going to force myself to take massive action forward, was if I didn't have a safety net. The heavy shame of feeling like a failure and blaming myself for not being able to provide my most basic needs of food, clothing, and shelter in the recent years had been keeping me stuck in a state of helplessness but this time

I was resolved to get it together for good. It was go-time. My friend had been through horrible abuse in her childhood and also earlier adult relationships, yet as her now husband describes her, "It's as if she is unaffected by the dark forces in the universe." She is a fierce, loving warrior woman. She knows how to own her reality. Nothing gets her down. No matter what happens to her, she always picks herself up and makes her way forward, usually making everyone laugh in the process.

My Ally helped me brainstorm new possibilities and she made me laugh a lot. My heart needed the laughter so badly. Being in her presence, feeling her attitudes and perspectives of life for a couple days, renewed my faith that I could get through the struggle. She encouraged me not to let the woman I was staying with push me around just because I was staying with her and felt indebted to her. About ten days later, I was on my way to Portland, determined to succeed no matter what it took.

Sometimes you might also find an Ally in an unexpected place.

Around the time I moved back to Portland just before the end of that year, I discovered that my former boyfriend from high school had recently relocated there. I would've never imagined him living in the Pacific Northwest, as he's Mid-west and Southern through and through. I ran into his mother while I was at my parents' house the month before and she mentioned it to him so he found my website and contacted me. We started writing emails and catching up on life.

He was still part of my life in 1998-99 when I moved to Philadelphia and lost most of my memories before that time. He was one of the only people who saw the before and after my first C-PTSD crash, though we didn't know what was happening to me at the time. We hadn't been in contact in over fifteen years and I had a lot of questions about what he remembered observing in me during that time. He had a lot of questions too, as the partners of people with PTSD/C-PTSD do. It's uncanny that he was guided back into my life to be there once again for me, this time during my last C-PTSD crash.

Once my friend and I were in the same city again, we started meeting for coffee and talking about life. I talked a lot about narcissistic abuse and at one point he said, "Wow, you really seem to understand this narcissist stuff!"

That's when my internal bell chimed. I realized that was it! I had finally found my niche in coaching. I don't know why it hadn't occurred to me to focus on narcissistic abuse, but sometimes we just need the nudge from someone else who can see it from outside and call it out.

I went back to the AirBnB where I was staying to update my website for this focus. For the next couple weeks, I stayed up until the wee hours of the night working on my new platform and starting to connect with other survivors of narcissistic abuse online. I realized how many people were going through it and how very similar the patterns were across the board. They were really grateful for my input so I knew I was on the right path.

After the New Year, I finally got into my new apartment and started creating content for my first YouTube videos and SANA webinars. One day just I sat in front of my computer, put aside my fears and recorded my first video ever. That one step of bravery and commitment was the beginning of a whole new direction in my life.

I am so grateful my trusted Ally showed up right when I needed his message to help me recognize what I needed to do at that moment. Without his observations, I might not have found my calling or my courage to step up. That one sentence he said was a pivotal moment in my recovery journey and stepping into a greater sense of my life purpose. More than just the words he said, he also believed in me, and that helped a lot.

Three of the Allies that will likely show up during the beginning of this stage are The Rock, The Nurturer, and The Shapeshifter[3].

I believe the most important one is the Rock, especially in the earlier stages of your recovery when you are deep in the storm of dread attacks, panic, fear and terror. This person needs to show up in your physical life. It's not going to work the same if you're having long-distance communication because you need to be able to feel this person's presence at this stage of your recovery. When you're near the Rock, you will feel the groundedness in their way of being there, listening to you or holding you, while your emotions are all over the place trying desperately to find solid ground.

It's important that you recognize this Ally is in your life to teach you something. Don't let yourself become dependent on them. Observe their ways of grounding emotionally and learn how to do that for yourself. This connection with your Rock is like wearing training wheels as you learn how to ground yourself through the storm and eventually find calmer territory, both internally and externally. Sometimes this Ally might need you just as much as you need them.

My friend from high school was like a rock during my first months back in Portland while I was going through the intense emotions after the C-PTSD crash, just as he had been in 1998-99 when it happened the first time, only this time I understood what was happening to me. I was trying to get on my feet again to move forward amidst the painful and overwhelming flashbacks from the past and the debilitating panic and dread attacks. Little by little I started to feel the solid ground beneath me and then my emotions became more grounded. Finally after several months, my work became more productive and focused and the brain fog had mostly cleared.

A few months into our renewed friendship, I quit smoking cigarettes for good. I had tried to quit many times over the years and managed to stay away for months at a time but I always went back to it. For some reason in March of 2016, one day I woke up and just didn't smoke.

Then the next day and the day after that. The rest of that pack of American Spirits sat in my drawer until I moved again almost a year later when I threw it away. I think in a way cigarettes were my rock. They were always there for comfort until I learned how to be my own rock through my friend's grounding example.

Eventually he opened up more about his relationship with his wife and it sounded like a classic abusive situation. The information and insights I gave him about narcissistic abuse helped him empower himself and stop blaming himself for what happened in their marriage. He learned how to set boundaries and deal with the mother of his children in healthier and more effective ways once he understood what she was doing. He stopped letting her walk all over him. He started finding himself again.

We both eventually left Portland. I'm not sure what force of nature allowed us to overlap there for that year but I am so very grateful for it. We are still good friends and Allies in this journey of life.

The Nurturer is the Ally who calms you down with encouraging, soothing words and compassion. This person has a lot of empathy and a generous spirit. If you're lucky you might know more than one Nurturer. This person has the ability to listen to you and tell you that everything is going to be alright. The Nurturer validates your feelings while encouraging you to take care of yourself.

The Nurturer teaches you to have compassion for yourself even in your worst moments.

If you've spent a lifetime giving your compassion endlessly to others, namely to abusive takers, you might realize you have an issue giving that same compassion to yourself. It's important not to become dependent on this Ally for nurturing, compassion and empathy but rather to learn how to do that more for yourself.

One of my other soul sisters is an incredibly nurturing presence in my life. We have known each other for eleven years. Though we've rarely lived in the same geographical area, we make the effort to see each other when we can, and with modern technology we are only a call or text away. She's gone through a lot of pain in her life and she has developed a sense of compassion like no one else I've ever met.

When anyone else is in pain, she is suddenly switched on in full nurturing mode. She radiates love and compassion that is nourishment for the soul and somehow that makes the pain more bearable. She validates feelings and makes helpful suggestions. Many people are unable to be present with others' pain, whether physical or emotional, because it makes them uncomfortable. That's what makes Nurturers stand out like diamonds in the rough.

She has comforted and inspired me with her nurturing presence on the phone every time I've been in awful, painful situations like when I fled the devastation in Peru and then faced a lot of adversity trying to get settled again in Portland, overcoming the C-PTSD crash landing. I'm so grateful for her nurturing presence in my life. She taught me how to be more compassionate to myself.

The Shapeshifter is an interesting character in the story. This Ally has the ability to appear in many forms and walk in many worlds, not necessarily physically though sometimes that's true but mostly in an energetic and emotional sense. This Ally may also contribute to a change in your environment, simply by being in your presence. The Shapeshifter can help you gain internal strength and wisdom, while showing you how to flow in various environments and places and around certain types of people.

*The Shapeshifter teaches you to develop
a greater sense of self-honesty.*

Observing how the Shapeshifter behaves slightly different in social interactions with certain people can help you gain the awareness and ability to do this yourself. This isn't about manipulation but rather protection. The Shapeshifter teaches you how to show up depending on the place and people involved, in other words, what parts of your true self you want to reveal to particular people and circumstances. Essentially, the Shapeshifter teaches you an important social filter (boundaries) that until this point you may have lacked.

If you grew up in a narcissistic household, you likely learned you had no right to boundaries and perhaps you were coerced into saying and doing what you didn't want to, pushed to say yes after saying no multiple times, and/or forced to share things that you wanted to keep private. After that kind of abuse training, which often continues into adulthood, eventually you stop being honest with yourself about what your needs are and what is okay with you, and that is what sets you up for more abusive relationships. The Shapeshifter teaches you how to up-level your self-honesty by setting and enforcing boundaries that create a safe container for your peace and wellbeing.

A Shapeshifter in my life taught me that real relationships allow for real truth and vulnerability, however superficial relationships like minimal contact and Gray Rock communication with toxic people require a certain trickster energy where you learn what you can share of yourself and what you can't in those relationships. There were many Tests during the first year of setting new boundaries with toxic people in general and especially with my mother. I would fail and get back up again several times.

My Shapeshifter friend related this trickster energy to desert dwellers. Because of the hostile environment, the animals and insects that live in the desert require trickster energy for survival. They often camouflage or pretend to be something they're not to avoid predators. Distinguishing between trick and truth is a matter of life or death. When she said that I immediately saw the parallel between the desert life and dealing with toxic people.

In a utopian world we'd never have to deal with another predator again, however in real life you'll find that they're all around and it's inevitable that they will cross your path here and there over a lifetime.

The wisdom you learn from the Shapeshifter will help you to manage yourself and your boundaries around toxic people and situations when going No Contact isn't an option or you're not ready for it yet, and also in the cases where you start to get entangled with a new toxic person and suddenly realize you need to set boundaries and high-tail it out of there.

Quite a few tests with manipulators showed up over the next year and every time they did I would get advice from my Shapeshifter friend on how to set the boundaries. She has taught me just about everything I know about boundaries and I'm so grateful for her wisdom.

Every time you advance another level, you'll likely find that you've called in a new Ally. Approach cautiously because at first you may not know if this is an Ally, an Enemy or a Test.

When life is trying to give you a nudge to shift and you're resisting that inner shift, you'll find that more Enemies and Tests keep showing up. The universe is not punishing you. It's pushing you to grow.

I spent the greater part of a year continuing to weather the storms, working hard to overcome the past and build a better future. My business was growing and I was feeling a new sense of passion and purpose in my life. For the first time in my life I felt like I was really making a difference in people's lives and that was filling my heart with joy like never before. At one point I made the mistake of sharing that joy on the phone with my mother, only to receive a birthday card in the mail a few weeks later with a Mother Teresa quote, her covert, sophisticated way of telling me that I should stop thinking big. "Not all of us can do great things. But we can do small things with great love." This is how we see you living your life. Her abuse is as thoughtful as the gifts she picks out for people.

I dated a couple people a few months apart, and within a few weeks each time found myself in toxic situations again, so I ended things quickly. I met a few new friends, most of whom also turned out to be toxic. I found the strength to go No Contact with several toxic family members, some who were quite close to me in the past. I met some toxic and manipulative people through my professional life who I also had to end contact with.

I was saying no a lot more than yes and that started to make a big difference in the quality of my daily life. Meanwhile I also strengthened my connection with several wonderful people already in my life. While some of the lessons were quite challenging, I was feeling more and more clear and confident about who belongs in my life and who doesn't. I became comfortable spending most of my time alone. Instead of focusing on the loneliness, I worked hard to build my business and live my purpose.

In June of 2016, I went to confront my mom on her abuse. She had nothing but covert aggressive tactics and excuses, ending the conversation with a spectacular performance for my dad and I about how much she loves gaslighting. I had hope that the conversation would change things but nothing changed, only her tactics became more sophisticated and she mostly stuck to the love-bombing for a while. I finally started recognizing her idealization for the superficial emptiness that it is, intended simply to pull me back in, only to put me down again in very meticulous and sophisticated ways, always with the plausible deniability factor absolving herself of any responsibility.

After that, I had minimal phone calls with my parents every other month, and inevitably afterward I would feel icky after talking with my mother. Whether it was her subtle digs or her fake, gushing support, or my dad laughing along at her histrionics and covert abuse, it all just felt icky.

I spent the holidays alone as usual with my dog. I enjoyed my peace, surrendering to the loneliness and feeling so grateful for all the positive changes that had taken place during that challenging year after my return to Portland. It's amazing how much changed in a year as I progressed through test after test, and kept moving forward. I looked at each test as an opportunity to practice my boundaries and build strength.

Over a year had passed after the last C-PTSD crash and things were pretty stable in my business and recovery. I started feeling like it was time to move abroad again, however this time without having to depend on a job or anyone else, running my business from my laptop. I planned my move for several months however I kept it all a secret from everyone but a few close, trusted friends and my coach. I didn't announce it to my parents until the last minute in order to avoid any negative energy from poisoning my process. I was rocking the boundaries and protecting my joy and dreams for the future.

Within the first three weeks of moving to a little town in Mexico, I already had more of a support network than I had in the three total years I lived in Portland. There were still some challenges yet I felt like I was on the right track. I was starting to feel freer and more at peace.

The learning experiences during this phase might go on for some time and this particular phase of Stage Two might be the longest of the whole journey. Experiences will test your progress, pushing you to keep reaching for the next level. A lot of those tests will come in the form of interactions with other abusive people. Abusive people will keep showing up for a while in ways that you have to deal with them until you deal with your emotional stuff. The more you clear out that emotional residue, the less they show up, the quicker you recognize them, and the more repelled they are from you. Every time you say no thank you to an abusive person, you're solidifying your stance to the universe that you will not tolerate abuse.

You might also find that the more you heal yourself, abusers and manipulators show up in more peripheral proximity to you, for a shorter time, and you don't have to deal with them long-term or on an intense, everyday basis like before. Noticing the drastic reduction in abusers showing up in your life, your ease in getting away from them ASAP, and better people entering the picture, shows that you're well on your way through this stage. During **(7) The Approach to the Innermost Cave⁴**, you'll be preparing to make another massive shift. This cave can be an actual physical location in your life where there is danger to your physical or psychological wellbeing, or it could be a deep inner conflict which you haven't had to face until now. It could also represent both. During this Approach you'll notice the ways in which you are **Inauthentic⁵** in your life. Essentially you're **Meeting Your False Self**.

You'll see one or more of your flaws staring you in the face. This is an opportunity to recognize the inauthenticity gap between how you are presenting yourself to the world (your identity) and who you really are (your essence).

This shift will likely take place through interpersonal relationships or it could be a life event of *force majeure*. However it comes about, something will suddenly reveal to you how you are being inauthentic in your life, and you'll have the opportunity to shift yourself into alignment with your integrity.

One night in late April 2017, now living in a small town in the central sierra of Mexico, I was watching a series on my laptop in bed. I kept feeling like I was kicking around a leaf or something crunchy between the sheets. I don't know why I didn't investigate. Perhaps I preferred the comfortable denial of "it's just a leaf" or "it's just a piece of granola" when neither of those in my bed really made rational sense.

It was dark and I was getting sleepy. Suddenly from under the sheets emerged something between me and the laptop. I was about to swat at it when I caught a glimpse of the curled tail in the glare from the screen. I didn't know I could jump that high or that fast from a horizontal position.

It ran under my laptop to hide. I turned the lights on, found my glasses and lifted the computer. Sure enough, it was a copper-colored scorpion now running to hide between my pillows. I went down to the utility room for the broom and dustpan on a broomstick. I stood with the broom in my hand in a warrior stance until I psyched myself up for the task of lifting the pillow and stabbing the venomous creature. I killed it, literally in the spot where I was laying just a few minutes before. The adrenaline was still coursing through my blood for hours later and every time I thought about the scorpion I had head to toe chills. On one hand I felt bad because I thought it didn't sting me but on the other hand, this was a venomous creature in my home and in my bed, and that was totally unacceptable.

Several days later I received text messages from my mother after a comfortable long period of silence since I had moved abroad. The next day a sharp burning, itching sensation began on my chest and right armpit. Nothing appeared on the skin, which was odd because they felt like strong electrical impulses. So I tried to ignore it.

Several days later, I had just moved into my new apartment after a couple months of moving around in temporary places. In my excitement, I texted my dad about my new apartment and he immediately asked to talk. I made the mistake of phoning my parents and sharing my joy about my new place. They caught me off guard and said they wanted to visit. Actually my dad was the negotiator and my mom said nothing while he asked me not *if* they could come visit, but when would be better, October or November, for them to visit. They wanted to stay with me since I had the space in my new place. I agreed and immediately wished I hadn't. I had promised myself that I'd never sleep in the same house as my mother again and just days before, I was considering going No Contact with her. Now suddenly they were planning on coming to visit. *Shit!*

Even though I wished I had said no, I felt strong at

the time of the phone call and I was telling myself that I could do it. I was assuring myself that she could be there for several days and I could manage the boundaries even though I didn't like the idea.

The next day I woke up to find my chest and right armpit broken out in a red burning, itching rash. It was so ugly and embarrassing not to mention incredibly uncomfortable. I felt like I was still wearing her shame, the shame of her abuse, which she has never owned and only made excuses for when I called it out the year before. I tried to cover up the rash with clothing and pretended it wasn't happening. I just wanted it to go away.

I didn't have internet at home yet so there were no distractions at night from feeling the gnawing bite of that rash. Feeling anxious and irritated wasn't helping so after fighting it a while I laid down to surrender into it. Any time pain or issues come up in my body in response to the psychological stresses, I eventually remember to lay down and start breathing. That's when I start to connect with the messages my subconscious is trying to convey through my body.

In my meditation that night I realized the areas of the rash corresponded to the heart meridian in Chinese Medicine (in the armpit) and the high heart or eighth chakra in the energetic system (on the chest) as well as the immune system (over the thymus gland). The heart is my joy, passion, connection and love. The immune system is my defense, my boundaries. I wasn't guarding my heart.

While reflecting on how I tried to cover up the rash when I went out in public, I had a flashback of having put concealer on the red blotch around the bug bite that I had above my left ankle when I went out to brunch with my adoptive mom the week before. I remembered the moment I had scratched it bloody open because it itched so bad and then I beat myself up for not having the self-control to leave it alone. I was trying to cover up layers and layers of shame and self-blame. *Holy denial, Batman!*

I started breaking through the denial and asked around about the inflamed area above my left ankle. I discovered that what I thought was a strange mosquito bite from the day before I found the scorpion, was in fact a scorpion sting. I was sharing a bed with it for at least two days! That explained the rash, which was the venom being excreted through my skin, exactly how my body often responds to toxins. It's odd that it delayed erupting until the emotional stress of the phone call with my mother more than a week later. The scorpion sting also explained the occasional stabbing pains in my liver area the first week after it happened as well as the tension in my neck and the painful numbness down the under side of my right arm for a few days the following week. My subconscious mind was suppressing it, just like it was suppressing the shame that I felt about the abuse in order to maintain a relationship with my mother. Eventually my body couldn't contain the stress any more and that's when I was forced to face it.

Two weeks after it happened, the scorpion sting wound wasn't getting better. I was still trying to ignore it for a while, until one night I had a dream that I had my left leg, where the sting was, in my mother's lap. In the dream, I brought up her abuse and she said, "Well if that's the way it's gonna be then I'm done with this." I understood that the only terms of having even a minimal relationship with her involved me pretending like everything is fine and to keep swallowing the abuse. That was no longer okay with me. I took my leg back and left.

Scorpion spirit animal is about boundaries, protection, death/rebirth and transformation. I realized I need to protect my heart more. I wasn't standing in my integrity because I was still pretending everything was fine with her, as she would like me to. Agreeing to allow her to visit was not going to be good for my health, wellbeing and sanity because it would mean that I would stuff down my feelings to make her feel comfortable, while she pretended nothing was happening. Pretending makes the heart suffer and eventually it gets sick. I could suddenly see the trajectory laid out in front of me and that path was no longer acceptable for me.

The point where the sting happened is around Gallbladder 39 in Chinese Medicine. Gallbladder energy is about decision-making and judgment. This particular point corresponds to neck tension and pain, common psycho-somatic symptoms I've had over the years due to frustration and anger. This point is also used to subdue Liver yang, and "hyper-excited indignation," representing the anger I had buried from decades of abuse because at some level I knew that the shame I had internalized wasn't mine to carry. The scorpion sting brought it all up to the surface.

After fully breaking through the denial about the scorpion sting, I was ready to look closer at the wound. The venom was still in my skin and the area was looking increasingly infected so I used organic baking soda and hot compresses to draw the venom to the surface. I was then able to rip out the white plug where it gathered into a point. I used hydrogen peroxide to clean the wound several times daily for about six weeks. It turned purple and scary for a while but I knew everything was going to be okay. I also felt like there was still something missing to make the inflammation go away.

Suddenly one morning when I woke up, the courage hit me and I texted my dad to say we needed to put their trip on hold until I figured some things out. I was buying time until I could make the inevitable decision. Around that time I felt like I needed something from the local environment to finally heal the sting wound. My adoptive mom gave me a piece of her local aloe plant and after one treatment, the wound made a drastic turn around. The inflammation started backing off. Eventually I forced myself to go in deeper and rip out the layer of necrotic tissue lining the wound. It was brutally painful and disgusting but it was totally worth it. I finally had a normal, healing wound.

Once I dug into the root of the wound, it got a lot worse before it got better, but it eventually healed and left only an ugly purple scar. I feel blessed that it wasn't any worse. One of my friends suggested a putting a tattoo there someday. I just might do that. Maybe it will be a scorpion or something to remind me of the lesson. The whole process was like a metaphor of the healing journey after narcissistic abuse.

The ugly and painful, yet powerful gift of the scorpion was a wake-up call. Like the scorpion, the venomous sting of narcissistic abuse is often not immediately recognizable, especially when we dissociate the pain and internalize the shame. Sometimes the side effects due to the toxicity are overwhelming yet difficult to connect to the root of the problem when you don't know what the root of the problem is or when you do but you just don't want to face it because the denial is more comfortable... until one day it's painfully clear and you're forced to deal with it.

I was out of integrity with myself because if one of my clients were telling me that story, I would strongly recommend No Contact with the mother yet I wasn't putting that into practice myself. I gave into the familial guilt and had agreed to the visit thinking I would just manage the boundaries and it would be okay. It took the scorpion medicine to force me to make a decision to prioritize my health, sanity and wellbeing.

I was out of integrity with myself by continuing to have a relationship with a person who never acknowledged what she did and had not changed in a year after the conversation in which I addressed her abuse. Were she any other person in my life, I would have cut her out years ago. The only reason I was giving her a pass was because she was my mother. However, trying to maintain that relationship even at minimal contact, was also keeping me locked in the trauma bond and shame. I knew what I had to do to get back into integrity with myself, and while I had made the internal decision, I wasn't ready yet to take action.

It might be that you avoid facing this inner issue of authenticity for a while. It's humbling and not very fun to face. You may also need some time to reflect on your journey and prepare for the challenges that you know are ahead of you. It might take some time for you to summon your inner courage to push through this test because it can be really challenging. There will be many temptations to give up along the way. If you persevere, you'll discover that every time you face and conquer another obstacle, you gain deeper insights into yourself and life while increasing your confidence and self-esteem. Whether or not you summon the humility and courage to move forward from here is up to you.

You will only step forward once you've fully accepted that your point of inauthenticity is hurting you. That sobering realization forces you to make a decision to change.

You might feel like you've hit a plateau or impasse at this point in Stage Two until someone else or another event of *force majeure* serves as a catalyst forcing you to look at yourself in a new way so you can take massive action and cross the Second Threshold.

Chapter 10
Crossing The Second Threshold

(8) The Ordeal[1] is the Second Threshold. It is the turning point of Stage Two where you are **Confronted**[2] by what you most fear, that which holds the ultimate power over your life. It may be a dangerous physical test of strength or a deep inner crisis that you face in order to move forward.

This moment is when you get to the bottom
of what's been holding you back.

It's ugly, I'm not going to lie, but it's worth facing so you can move through it. This crisis has a certain life or death feeling even if your physical life isn't at risk. The ego often experiences a symbolic death when you make a massive upgrade in your sense of self.

This is the death and rebirth of your old self into your new self
where you face your greatest fear or deadly enemy.

In order to overcome this difficult challenge of **Facing Your Fear**, you'll need to draw upon all your skills and wisdom of experience.

While the scorpion sting reality was unraveling, a friend of some acquaintances of mine in Peru contacted me online and we started talking. He found me right in that point of vulnerability.

Immediately he asked when I was going to visit Peru again. I said never and told him I left too much trauma and pain there when I fled in October of 2015.

I was afraid to see the abusers and the places that

reminded me of everything that happened. However, I also really wanted to be able to take small groups of people there for retreats to work with the plant medicines in their recovery after narcissistic abuse. By not facing my fear, I was letting the past hold me back from the future that I wanted to create.

Over the next several weeks, that guy kept asking when I was going to Peru. His insistency helped me accept that I had to go back to clear the past, to reclaim the spaces, and to stand in my courage and strength if I ever wanted to be able to open that door for others. I decided this was the sign that it was time to go face what had happened there in the past and I knew it was all somehow connected to the mother wound.

I was terrified but ready so I bought the ticket and reserved the hotels, departing in two weeks. It wasn't the first time I booked an international trip within weeks of departing. While that might sound crazy to some, those intuitive travel impulses had always led me to the people and places that helped catalyze massive transformations in my life. I was fully trusting in my decision, come what may.

You might feel like everything that matters to you is on the line at this point. Until now you haven't addressed this issue in your life because you haven't had to.

This threshold is the turning point in your character transformation.

You've been avoiding making this change until now because it's scary and maybe even seems unattainable. Eventually it becomes suddenly so clear that you cannot continue forward on the healing journey without addressing this fundamental issue.

Essentially this is another wake-up call where you accept that you must change. I can guarantee that your ego won't go down without a fight. Mine didn't either. It went kicking and screaming!

Standing at this threshold, I discovered that my ego was so terrified of feeling unsafe and getting deceived again, that I was projecting the past experiences onto the present. I was unable to see what was actually in front of me because all I saw was fear. I was confused and unsure what was going on because there was so much fear clouding my radar.

I was gaslighting myself and continuing to create a reality that I didn't want to live in. Since the scorpion and phone call the month before, I was in an almost constant state of fear and panic at night and at times during the days. I felt so unsafe. I wasn't letting myself see the present opportunity for growth in front of me because I was too scared to be wrong or hurt.

In order to not feel unsafe any more, I had to be willing to feel totally unsafe, to surrender to that feeling instead of pushing it away but I didn't understand this yet.

I was so overwhelmed by the fear and panic that I wasn't sure what was my intuition and what was my fear. I was having deep self-doubts that I hadn't felt in a long time and that was only contributing to the overwhelming sense of fear. My self-trust had grown so much over the last year and a half, yet suddenly I was so unsure of myself again. My fears were trapping me in the past and blocking me from taking the necessary risks in order to experience a whole new reality.

Through the mirror of that guy who pushed me to go back to Peru, I was able to see myself in ways I couldn't alone, wrapped in my blanket of false security at home. While I was there, he called me out on my fear and panic, every step of the way. He was right about most of it and I couldn't deny it. He didn't let me get away with it. He didn't baby me. Instead he challenged me to better myself and he didn't accept weakness as an answer without calling it for what it was, thereby encouraging me to step up and summon my courage where it was lacking.

I was ashamed of my fear. Six months ago, a year ago,

his pushiness for me to face my fear would have scared me away and pissed me off because I wasn't ready for that message yet. It was finally time and for whatever reason I called in a tough teacher as a guide to cross this threshold. Everything happens in its time and for a reason, at least that's how I choose to see life because it's the only way that I can make sense of things.

There were moments during that week when I didn't want to go through it. I just wanted to hide, curl in a ball and cry like a little girl rather than face my fears. But I knew I couldn't do that. The only alternative was to return unchanged after having risked nothing, and therefore let down everyone including myself. That was not an option I was willing to live with.

A couple of nights there I worked with *wachuma*, a psychedelic cactus and the South American cousin of peyote. During the last experience on the last night, I finally saw clearly inside myself what that guy had been trying to show me the whole time, which my ego was fighting all the way.

I realized that in order to fully pass this threshold of the self-healing journey after narcissistic abuse, I had to surrender my ego's attachment to the false sense of security that I had created through isolation and not risking my heart in relationships.

My biggest fear was being deceived again by a relationship and feeling unsafe. This was my biggest life lesson that I had repeated over and over again with abusive people.

As I was internally processing all of this, the guy said to me, "Your desire to heal must be stronger than your ego." *Shit*. Those were the biting words that invited my ego to release its attachments to the fear and wound. That's when the new revelations began to unravel.

I had to surrender my ego's desire to control my safety by hiding, avoiding, and fearing. It was time for me to venture out with courage in my heart, knowing that I am protected because I have much better boundaries now than before.

I had to be willing to surrender my ego's story about my wound from narcissistic abuse and allow it to be over instead of looking for it everywhere by projecting fear.

I had to be willing to let go of the fight in my head with my mother and trying to get her to acknowledge that what she did and still does is abusive. I had to let go of wanting her to admit that she is abusive.

I had to let go of hoping things would ever be different with her or that I could fix it.

I had to be willing to stop trying to have a relationship with my mother because the only terms of that relationship would be if I kept internalizing the shame and pretended like everything was fine. That was no longer an option if I wanted to move past this threshold.

I had to be willing to stop looking for others' validation on this matter and stop getting upset, like when that guy said that I needed to forgive and love my mom for who she is because she's my mother. I had to be willing to stand firmly in my own reality and do what I know I need to do for my own wellbeing no matter what others think.

I had to surrender my ego's reliance on, "that's just my PTSD" as an excuse when I didn't want to grow to the next level. It was time to grow. I was ready to let go.

It was time to release the fear, the illusion, the hope, the heartbreak, the shame. The *wachuma* ceremony that night felt like a little funeral. Something definitely died inside me.

It was hard to let go, even of the awful stuff. I realized that the ego likes the wounds. It's attached to them because the wounds give us a sense of identity and familiarity. Letting go of the attachment to the wound in a weird way feels like losing a long-term companion.

My ego did not give it up and go down without a fight. I was struggling, going back and forth with myself for hours through this process until I finally surrendered.

When the shift finally happened, I could feel a house of cards fall down and in its place, a new growing sense of peace and relaxation setting in.

I stayed up most of the night processing the feelings and revelations, mostly about my mother. I finally stopped fighting with her in my head. I stopped defending myself and my perspective of reality and worrying about what she or anyone else in the family thought. I no longer felt attached to her reality and I no longer had the desire to try to make someone else understand why a daughter would not want anything to do with her mother. I officially had no more fucks to give. It felt so matter-of-fact that it was almost anti-climatic after all this time and all the struggle.

The trauma bond had been weakening for some time and it was finally broken. Soft tears of relief, joy and gratitude rolled out the sides of my eyes until I fell asleep.

As you cross this threshold, the fear and terror has been noticeably neutralized. Previously, there was still intense emotion connected to an abuser, evoking an intense emotional reaction.

The Second Threshold is the turning point where you stop letting the fear and panic control you unconsciously. At this threshold of recovery from narcissistic abuse, you are invited to let go of an enormous amount of fear and panic which is holding the trauma bond in place, even if by a thread by this point.

The fear is the glue of the trauma bond.

The shattering of the trauma bond is a spontaneous moment. You can't force it but you can help yourself get there by continually and relentlessly facing the truth, and when this moment of reckoning with your fear shows up, have the courage to step through the threshold.

This threshold will often come about through a relationship or interaction with another person. You will have the opportunity to release the false security that you've built up during the earlier stages of healing that allowed your ego to feel safe but then eventually was actually holding you back from growing further. The false sense of security was like your training wheels.

As you cross the Second Threshold, a new era of peace and calm begins and this is another almost tangible feeling that you can measure. You'll notice greatly diminished fear, terror and panic. When the fear does come on after this it's only momentary and it feels so foreign. Until this point perhaps your entire life you were plagued by fear and terror, and maybe you didn't even notice because you were so used to it. It's like noticing the noise the refrigerator is making only when it abruptly stops.

This is the doorway where many people stay stuck and repeating the past before moving forward. I did for quite some time. It's not that I didn't know the truth consciously, it's just that until this point my subconscious wasn't fully on board yet.

This breakthrough is a sudden, visceral understanding of your truth and a new inner strength to not go back to an abuser, to release the toxic hope, and to be able to recognize, pick up and leave immediately anytime you find another manipulator in your life.

When your ego is ready to surrender, your inauthentic identity will implode, revealing your true essence. This moment may surprise you and catch you off guard. It might even be scary to let go of who you were.

At this point you may need to burn some bridges
in order to keep yourself from going back to what hurts you.

In one cycle of transformation you might experience this threshold with a person you were in an adult relationship with while perhaps simultaneously you're working through another larger cycle of transformation regarding the trauma bond connecting you to one of your parents or caretakers, your original abuser. There are multiple layers to the journey of self-healing.

The big kahuna is when the trauma bond to the original abuser in your life shatters, completely dissolving your present desire to connect with him/her or any other abusers from your past as well as any desire to engage with new manipulative characters who show up in your present life. Before this moment you probably noticed how you were attracted to abusive types and now as you move forward you'll notice how you feel repelled and repulsed by them.

Abusers are often hoovering and hitting all the emotional points to try to pull you back after you cut your emotional energy off from them. They want your missing energy supply because it feeds them and they're addicted to that. It's tempting to react when they hit your deepest wound with their words of seduction or cruelty but now you're seeing it all from a new perspective which makes it a lot easier to opt out.

You may realize at this threshold that what actually had the greatest power over your life was not the person but the feeling they evoked in you, which was repeated via other people throughout your life. Pay attention to the feeling. That's the wound. It's internal. Your ego will try to convince you that it's external.

If you resist crossing the Second Threshold, you'll eventually find yourself in a breakdown that leads to a downward spiral and return to earlier healing stages or another abusive relationship. Eventually it will lead you back to this doorway and, when you're ready, into a breakthrough.

The breakdown cycle will continue in drama after drama
until you drop your inauthentic self, your false self.
Your authenticity is what cuts through the denial.

Essentially when you stop lying to yourself you can do what you know you need to do without all the confusion and doubt in the way. Face the stark reality and keep facing it relentlessly until you break through.

If you're stuck at this threshold trying to get past the doorway, stop yourself from indulging in the illusion, the fantasy of what you wish it was or what you hoped it would be. Focus on reality. Face the truth relentlessly. Step into the courage when you are invited to confront the fear.

Signs that you're still in the trauma bond are:

- you're still hoping for or still accepting contact from people who hurt you because maybe they will apologize or change
- you're still helping people who have hurt you out of guilt or a sense of obligation
- you're still extending trust to people who have showed you over and over again that they are not trustworthy
- you still can't cut off from toxic relationships of the past
- you're still attracted to new toxic people that you meet
- you're still trying to convince abusive people in your life that there's a problem with their behavior and yet they are unable to accept self-responsibly for their actions
- you're still defending your decision and/or looking for approval and validation from other people to tell you whether you have the right to cut off an abusive person
- you're still fighting with abusive people in your head, defending yourself against their accusations and arguing with their reality paradigm
- you're still afraid of the abuser

Chapter 11

After the Second Threshold

You will feel like a new person as you emerge from the battle at the Second Threshold. Now you can extract the nectar of the experience, which often comes in the form of new insights and understandings. Sometimes this treasure is represented in the physical world but often it's more symbolic and internal.

This is where you redefine yourself again. You enter **(9) The Reward**[1] having shed your biggest inner obstacle to integrity and generated a greater sense of empowerment, strength and insight into yourself and your life. The old ego dies to be **Reborn**[2] and you are able to receive the treasure. Now that the shame has died with the trauma bond, this is where you embrace **Self-acceptance**.

This is your reward for persevering through your greatest personal challenge. A deep inner conflict (the trauma bond) that until now was draining so much of your energy has suddenly neutralized and disappeared. This re-energizes your motivation to keep moving forward.

Once your ego and character shift, you'll see new meaning in the past events. You'll begin to accept yourself and your decisions. A sense of peace and calm will penetrate your daily life and your memories of the past. You'll discover more about your own authenticity, your true self in the here and now. You might even catch a glimpse of the essence of the universe... the feeling of oneness and unity, and a deep knowing that you are part of everything.

After my revelations with *wachuma* that night, I saw the three stages of recovery from narcissistic abuse clearly for the first time. I realized I needed to write a book on this topic. I expedited the priority level to the front of my dashboard for the next month. It was time to clarify this process to myself so I could share this treasure with others.

I had seen the general outline of the three stages for some time but I couldn't fully see the scope before that night because even though I had been thriving in many ways with my work, my sense of contribution and life purpose as well as my dedicated self-care practices and blooming self-love, I didn't realize that I hadn't yet fully moved into the Thriving Stage regarding the original abuser (my mother) until after that night in the Andes Mountains when my ego finally surrendered. My whole life changed after that night, in ways that weren't really visible right away though I could definitely feel the difference internally.

The terror and panic that had ramped up since the scorpion sting and phone call was suddenly gone. I felt an unfamiliar lightness inside myself. It was such a relief! I realized that the fear of heartbreak had been with me since childhood. That was my deepest wound. It was always there and now it was no longer. I felt like I had been reborn the morning after the *wachuma* ceremony.

I headed to the airport and on the long journey home I reflected on the experiences during the last ten days. My energy was no longer connecting with the feeling of heartbreak nor the fear of it.

When the fear dissolved, the shame died too. That shame and fear that I'd been carrying as long as I could remember had been blocking a healthy sense of worthiness. Now without it, I was starting to experience a new level of joy in my life. Internally there was a massive shift, even though nothing seemed to have shifted externally yet.

I wasn't sure what was going to happen once I went back home to my daily life to integrate this new breakthrough but I knew that everything had changed for the better now and the ripples were spreading outward.

At this point you will now know deep inside yourself that you are worthy. You'll feel this internally. You'll also see this reflected in your interactions with other people and the world around you.

You'll notice a new level of self-acceptance emerge
as you release the enormous weight of toxic shame
with the trauma bond.

Anything that doesn't resonate with your new sense of worthiness will suddenly become so obvious, and that is precisely what opens the door to the Third Threshold.

Chapter 12

Crossing The Third Threshold

At the end of Stage Two and marking the transition into Stage Three is the Third Threshold. Even though you'll feel an immense release of fear, tension and shame along with an increase in self-worth after crossing the Second Threshold, you'll quickly realize that you need to prepare for the last leg of this journey.

The Third Threshold represents **(10) The Road Back**[1]. A new challenge shows up to test your dedication to your healing, growth and purpose. You might feel **Desperate**[2] at this point when you come to a sudden and daunting realization that makes your path forward challenging. You might find yourself in a tight spot between the proverbial rock and a hard place. This is **The Dilemma**.

This opportunity gives you something new to fight for.

It's also the Law of Verification. As soon as you make a massive shift, the universe tests you by offering you the same challenge again. How you respond tells the universe whether you're sure you want that or not. It's a way of proving that you've transformed yourself in some way and clearing old patterns for good. The universe is constantly pushing us to transform because this is a fundamental characteristic of life.

On the way home from the Mexico City airport returning from Peru the day after the massive release of fear and panic, the universe tested me so I could prove to myself that I was done with that.

About an hour into the four hour drive to the small town where I lived, I woke up to realize my driver and I were stuck at a standstill on the highway. It was 2:34 AM. The trucks surrounding us already had their engines and lights off. There was an eerie, dark silence. My driver got out to find out what was going on. He heard that PEMEX trucks were transporting something and the highway would be closed until 6 AM. For a second I saw the opportunity to start freaking out about a lot of things.

A Julio Cortázar short story that I'd read in college, *The Highway of the South* (*La Autopista del Sur*)[3] came to mind. I thought about the safety of the area at that hour. I thought about us there like a sitting duck for assault or robbery. I thought about if I never got home, would anyone even know...

There were a lot of fears I could have engaged with and in the past I definitely would have, but all of that faded into the oblivion without any energy loss. I decided not to invest my energy in the fears and instead I went to sleep. Compared to the prior months of difficulty sleeping from all the panic and fear, I was able to fall asleep immediately, albeit uncomfortably stretched across the back seat of the car.

I woke up at 4 AM when the car started moving again and the truck behind us was honking. Apparently the highway was reopened two hours earlier than anticipated. I recognized that was a Law of Verification test that the universe offered me. However, I didn't realize that this wasn't the big verification test yet. It was more of a warm-up.

This threshold and dilemma is often a massive transformation that you won't see coming, at least not in the way it takes place. Sometimes what you think you want in life ends up paling in comparison to the blessings this universe wants to give you — which is what you actually need.

When you give up what you think you want for what you actually need, even when you can't see proof of that yet, you release your ego desires and attachments so you can open to accept the gift that is waiting for you.

Right before this point, you maybe thought that you had it all figured out. Then suddenly you end up questioning yourself because a life event shows you that what you thought you wanted conflicts with what you actually need. This is likely when you are forced to see a person, relationship or situation in your life, now without the goggles of the trauma bond and fear. You'll have to choose between your growth and thriving or remaining in the toxic situation that you hoped would work out. It's one or the other. You can't have both.

Less than two weeks after returning from Peru, I had to go to the States to retrieve the rest of my stuff from storage and attend my soul sister's wedding. There was a crazy fiasco of massive ineptitude at the Dallas airport immigration process which almost caused me to miss my connecting flight to Portland. I had to sprint to the gate with my carry-on bag, greatly exacerbating the pain I had in my left rib cage and behind my heart from when the guy in Peru accidentally hurt me while trying to align my back. My legs almost didn't carry me the last 20 yards because my muscles were freezing up. I just barely made my flight and when I sat down I was feeling desperate for the excruciating pain to go away. I couldn't focus on anything else and I didn't know how I was going to be able to heavy lift boxes and suitcases for the next week.

The next morning in Portland, I was able to get a CBD tincture to make the inflammation and pain start to diminish immediately and that allowed me to pop the sprained rib behind my heart back in place after some movement and stretching.

I started to feel immense relief around the physical pain and that was quickly replaced with a feeling in my gut that something was going on with the guy, that he wasn't being honest. I had no proof so I decided not to address it. I focused on getting done the necessary tasks and then having fun with my friends at the wedding as well as my cousins in town.

That guy had simultaneously been traveling in his

country to work at a festival and at first it seemed only to be our traveling and the bad internet signal there that was creating a disconnection between us. I was busy working on coordinating a lot of details and nursing the rib so I was somewhat distracted from my feelings about it but at some level I knew something was off.

By the last day of my journey, he was also returning to his home. We were able to talk for a little bit on video and he told me he had kissed a woman there but that's all that happened. I nodded my head. He had already made it clear that we have no commitment to each other. I agreed due to the long distance, but this wasn't what I really wanted.

He said, "I hate when you do that with your head, it's like you don't care!" My stomach sank and I realized he was angry that I didn't give him narcissistic supply in the form of negative emotions like jealousy or sadness. He wanted me to get upset and I didn't. I started feeling queasy and began releasing my attachment to the future plans we had talked about. My stomach was confirming that it wasn't going to happen even though I didn't want to fully accept it because it didn't look that bad yet.

After I got home to Mexico, I was having a deep dilemma whether to keep giving him a chance or to end it without any real proof. That dilemma was sucking up my energy and causing me to watch entire seasons of TV series at night and on weekends instead of investing my energy in my passions and purpose. My ego desperately wanted things to work out with the fantasy I had but at the same time I knew something was off and I couldn't deny that to myself.

If I had to make the decision based solely on my own desire to be in a partnership and maybe even have a little family, I might have chosen to keep giving him a chance. At some level I knew that if I screwed up, if I made the wrong choice, I was going to get derailed from my purpose and mission and that was going to affect a lot more lives than just mine. The thought of that was sobering.

So I decided to let go of the fantasy. I stopped investing

energy in that and in him and instead redirected toward my work full throttle. The book was really coming along and I decided that's where I wanted to invest my energy so I kept cranking out the pages. The internal decision was made, the only thing left was the external execution.

You might want to pursue a love interest, friendship, work opportunity or other situation with manipulative characters because parts of it sound like what you wanted. However, now that you've released the heavy burden of toxic shame at the Second Threshold you know that the person or people involved can't treat you with the respect that you know you are worthy of, and since you've also reached a new level of integrity, which you are fiercely owning through your decisions and actions, you're unwilling to accept anything less.

At this point, if you don't remove yourself from the toxic person or situation, you will compromise your mission to thrive and contribute your gift to the world. This threshold is kind of like a reverse echo of the Call To Adventure[3] from Stage One. In Stage One you were starting to answer your personal calling and now as you are about to enter Stage Three you're able to apply your personal calling toward a greater contribution to the world around you. That is actually what encourages you to make the best decision at this threshold, because you know the choice you make here and now is much bigger than you.

This is the choose between your personal desires and a higher good. You might just want to hit the easy button and watch Netflix all day long, or go out and party every night with your friends after all the work you've been doing in this journey, but deep down you're realizing that you've got more work to do and it's time to rise to the occasion, no matter what anyone around you is doing or wants you to do.

What you want in this moment is something external and based on the ego desires, fear, security, money, safety, companionship, being right, winning, etc. What you need is something internal like self-love, self-trust, self-respect, growth and fulfillment.

It's a tough decision to let go of the ego's grip on what it thinks it wants.

Now that you have already confronted your inauthenticity at the Second Threshold, the choices you make at this point need to be in integrity with your true essence. You're no longer willing to sacrifice your integrity for something your ego thinks it wants, even if you consider it for a moment. You know what you need to do and you take action. This bolsters your self-trust.

When you make the choice based on your true self-expression, you will be able to release your ego's grip on what you thought you wanted, setting yourself free and opening the path for something wonderful to enter. While you can't see the future it yet, if you hold onto what you think you want, you will miss out on something so much better that is waiting for you to make this decision. By making the decision to honor your integrity and peace, the universe will reward you.

The decision you make at this threshold is
ultimately to protect your peace.
As you cross the Third Threshold your self-trust is restored.

As you abandon your attachment to your ego desires, which were previously in the way, you can now release an enormous amount of tension that was draining your energy.

You have gained a new sense of inner peace and calm, no matter what's going on around you. It's a lot easier to opt out of other people's dramas because you recognize immediately what an energy suck they are and you'd rather enjoy your peace.

The old reality starts falling away as you choose the new reality. It's one or the other, so if you aren't ready to let go of the old reality, you'll stay there to keep repeating lessons with increasing discomfort until you decide to release your grip on it and cross the threshold. It's not so easy to just let go of what you thought you wanted so don't beat yourself up if you aren't ready yet to enter Stage Three.

STAGE THREE

Thriver
Actualized
Reconnection

Chapter 13

Summary of Stage Three

Judith Herman writes, "Survivors whose personality has been shaped in the traumatic environment often feel at this stage of recovery as though they are refugees entering a new country."[1]

Stage Three is the reintegration phase
where you return as a new person.

In Stage Three you're now returning to your ordinary world as a changed person. The village (your city, town, family, community) has probably not changed much. However for you, it feels like a whole new reality compared to before the Third Threshold.

Everything feels foreign and weird when you return. Others expect you to be who you were when you left, but you've been through a massive transformation. Even the space around you in your home might feel foreign because you are internally different now. You're also reentering the places where you left behind the memories of the past. Now you're able to clear them and reset the grid with your new changes.

There will be temptations to return to your old self because it feels more comfortable than to go against the current and integrate the new you, your new reality. There will be tests to verify the transformations you made, but on the whole this stage is much, much easier than the previous two.

So much has changed inside you during the journey, so expect that things will start to change around you now to adjust to that shift. There might be sudden news and changes in your relationships, your home, your work, or other areas of your life. Be ready to surf the flow and notice how the universe always provides exactly what you need, even if not in the way you imagined.

New people will enter your life and you'll have opportunities to practice being yourself with them. Some will like you and some will not. Your new sense of self-trust and self-acceptance is no longer looking for their approval or acceptance.

Some people from your old life may not like your transformation because they can no longer get what they wanted from you with this new dynamic. Once again you may find yourself cutting out more toxic people from your life, the ones who were staying under the radar before the changes but now even they are feeling uncomfortable about your new sense of worthiness and self-trust so that naturally creates tension.

This tension will feel alarming now that you got used to a new level of inner peace and self-trust after the Third Threshold. Your internal alarm system proves to be functioning well now. You can quickly differentiate between a threat and a non-threat without questioning yourself like in the past.

You have a very different relationship with yourself now.

You're now integrating your transformations into your daily reality and you will start to see the sprouts coming to life. It is a whole new world now, like nothing you've experienced until this point. It will feel foreign but also home in a way.

Now as a thriver you are bridging the gap between the trauma and purpose and you are living with a new sense of life purpose on the daily. You are feeling like your contributions are making a difference in the lives of others. Your new filter for the boundary of NO is, *does this serve my purpose?*

Instead of all the heavy emotions of the past, your baseline state is now gratitude. As emotions come up, they'll pass and you'll notice the increased ease you have to shift back to gratitude.

This is the stage where you complete the circle. There's an ending of one cycle and a beginning of a new one, though you likely won't notice a hard line because it's all so connected and intertwined in the process of life.

Chapter 14

The Common Markers of Stage Three

- seeking new meaning in your life
- desire for reconnection with community
- new focus on your life dreams and goals
- spiritual/existential questions become a bigger focus than the past
- increasing insights and revelations into who you are and what you're here to do
- feeling a desire to contribute something to make a difference in the world around you
- new commitment and determination to your purpose-driven mission (you're now bridging the gap between the trauma and your purpose)
- your growing sense of purpose magnetizes you forward and out of the gravity of the past
- you feel lighter and your daily life no longer feels like such a drag (now that an enormous weight of the past has dissolved)
- you've released your false sense of security and now you're replacing it with a new level of trust (of yourself, others and the universe)
- the cloudiness of the past terror and panic is gone and replaced with a new clarity
- you don't feel the need to worry as much because you trust that if something is wrong, you'll know it and meanwhile you can enjoy life
- you've released the huge burden of toxic shame that you've carried for years if not all your life, you know KNOW that you're worthy and you see that reflected in your daily experiences

- you're fully owning your perception and your reality (and when you don't like it you know that you and only you can change it so you take new action)

- you feel more integrated and not fragmented like before

- you have new and more positive belief systems about yourself and life

- much more positive self-talk/Inner Dialogue (and the reprogramming of negative thoughts has now become integrated into your subconscious vs. having to consciously focus on it like before)

- you're living in a new reality, feeling a new sense of meaning in your life

- a new sense of peace and relaxation sets in

- with greater self-control and emotional equanimity, you no longer react emotionally as you used to (to other people and life events)

- much more able to let go of the little things that happen on the daily because the weight of the past is not triggered with every new frustration

- you're discovering the treasure in the trauma, some kind of gift that you now have and can use to help others

- you're developing new and deeper relationships (also more able to relate with people who didn't go through the abuse and don't really understand it)

- your new relationships are based on authenticity, integrity and reciprocal give/take (and if not you exit immediately with new strength and clarity than before)

- you're rebuilding your social skills and feeling more comfortable around others

- you may feel an occasional overwhelming sense of gratitude when you realize how far you've come and how different life is now compared to months and years before

- you're unleashing your joy like never before

- you're laughing and smiling a lot more

- you're recognizing the collateral damage of the abuse you endured (i.e. noticing the effects it had on your dog or kids, like their fear or anxiety) and you're making up for it now as best as you can, including practicing self-forgiveness

- you're starting to feel part of something, like you belong somewhere (and maybe for the first time in your life)

- increased sense of success in relationships and life

- new levels of abundance in all areas of your life (health, love, career, personal growth, friends, wealth and spirituality) which are now flourishing like never before

- increased resilience to difficulties that you encounter nowadays

- a deep sense of acceptance that what happened happened and it's okay now because you're finding ways to transmute the trauma into purpose

- you even look different, younger and more vibrant (people around you might notice this more than you do)

- increased sense of freedom of being

- you're much more present in the moment and able to envision, plan and take steps toward the future that you're creating in the present moment

- much greater ease of self-expression when you're alone and with others

- you often realize that life is a miracle

Chapter 15

The Work of Stage Three

Stage Three is about incorporating and integrating the lessons and insights from the journey into your life. It's also about reintegrating socially with the world around you.

New Choices

During this stage you're realizing that you have a lot more options than you saw before. Now you start to make new choices much easier because you've gained a lot of clarity, strength and confidence during the trials and tribulations of Stage Two.

During Stage Two you were noticing how you feel and validating those feelings. Mostly those feelings were unpleasant as you were processing your way through a lot of past gunk, purging and opening to new possibilities. In Stage Three it's important to focus on how your heart wants to feel, and working to put yourself in that state no matter what is going on around you. Your feelings are no longer hostage to the external events and people in your life.

When you don't feel good, now you can regulate yourself more efficiently with self-talk like, "I don't have to feel like that any more. How I feel is my choice. So how do I want to feel?"

When people tell us, "just let it go, leave it in the past," in Stage One this can feel very invalidating and it's not appropriate to the time and place in the journey. It's impossible to just let it go and leave it all in the past during the first stage because there is much questioning, understanding, processing, restructuring and revisiting to do. However, by the time you are entering Stage Three, "just let it go and leave it in the past" is exactly the choice that will lead you to truly thriving.

Owning Your Reality

You're feeling more assertive and you're owning your reality. When others try to gaslight you and cause you to doubt your perception of reality, you don't fall for it any more and you stop gaslighting yourself.

You trust yourself implicitly now.

You stand strong and confident against oppression and negativity no matter how others try to confuse you. You are also humble enough to recognize when your stuff comes up to work on and you keep working on it.

Planning for the Future

In this stage you're now able to really envision, dream and plan for the future that you want to live so you can keep moving in that direction.

*You're now much more focused on building
your future than revisiting the past.*

The past will come up a lot less frequently and when things do, they don't have nearly the emotional weight they had before. You'll notice the old emotions have been mostly neutralized. It's so much easier and quicker to move through things and shift yourself out of an unpleasant emotional state now without the gravity of the past.

You're tying up loose ends and dusting out the corners to prepare for what you are creating. You might go through a purge at some point to release the old emotional energy that was still hanging on in your body so you can step forward without it.

You're spending a lot more energy planning for the future and taking action in the present to get there, instead of dwelling on the past. You're much more interested in the future than the past as well. Most importantly, you believe in your ability to create the future you dream of.

A New Relationship with Fear

By now you're now looking at your old fears in a new way. It's like visiting your elementary school twenty years later and realizing how small it is when it seemed so big before. The building didn't change, you grew.

Keep facing your fears as they come up. You may want to have a catch phrase like, "no thank you!" or "back it up, bitch!" to keep those fears in check with a little humor as they surface. They will back off significantly quicker in Stage Three because you now feel safe.

Mostly the fears will pass by like empty thoughts without triggering an emotional response. This allows you to easily adopt the perspective of the Observer, your higher awareness that now recognizes the frequency of fear and panic, consciously deciding not to engage with it unless, of course, it's a matter of survival and the fear is necessary to get you to safety.

Growing Resilience

People will still test you in this stage but you'll no longer be reactive like in the past. That's not to say you won't feel hurt when people hurt you but you'll no longer fall into the trap of emotionally reacting to their bullshit. You'll see it and recognize it for what it is instead of losing your self-control and giving them your power.

When you no longer give away your power to people who attempt to rattle you by eliciting a negative emotional reaction, you also won't allow whatever they did or said to consume you afterward. Things may surprise you, but you'll quickly recognize what's happening and you'll have the mental strength to redirect your emotional power to how you want to feel instead of how others want you to feel in order to meet their supply demand. Your new emotional Teflon is letting it slide off you instead of sticking to you and getting internalized, which makes it easier to walk away from those people instead of feeling sucked into defending yourself.

During Stage Three it's much easier for you to shift into a positive state when something knocks you off balance.

In the prior stages when something knocked you off balance you'd fall down and have a hard time getting back up. You no longer go into that downward spiral. Now it's like tripping on something that you didn't see in the sidewalk and catching yourself gracefully as you keep walking forward.

Keep mastering the old traumatic experiences through controlled challenges (AKA prolonged exposure). These challenges are about voluntarily exposing yourself to what used to scare you in the past so you can keep reclaiming the places and activities that used to hold power over you. You'll notice how much quicker you'll be able to return to the places where you went with your ex, or watch the next season of the TV series you watched together, or face anything else that in the past would cause the sharp pangs of nostalgia and loss among other emotions.

Much like your new response to fear, you'll be able to see the memory and invitation to feel sad about the past but you will easily choose not to connect to that frequency and instead shift yourself into a feel-good state. Eventually there won't be any emotional residue associated with that person or place any more. Returning to those places with your new positive emotional state of growth is like clearing the energetic grid that you left behind and that has a holographic shift on your whole life.

Clarity of Purpose

In Stage Three you're focusing on gaining greater clarity around your sense of purpose and living your purpose. Your purpose is the expression of your soul in the world. It's your WHY. Your purpose is what most matters to you in life. It's not a goal or destination but rather something you live every moment of every day.

If you want to create lasting change in your life,
you've got to be tapped into your sense of purpose.

By this stage you'll be feeling much more driven by your purpose. Even when people try to derail your energy to put out their fires and respond to their false emergencies, you'll be able to stand strong and clear with your boundaries around your time and energy. With your sense of purpose as a filter, you'll be able to set the boundaries you need to in order to keep living your truth and focusing your energy on contributing your highest good to the world. In the past you would've felt a heavy dose of guilt in prioritizing yourself and your life's work but now you know this is the best thing you can do for yourself and those you are serving.

Occasional light pangs of false guilt might appear but you will be able to consciously remind yourself to let it go and focus on the truth. Sacrificing your energy and sense of purpose to meet someone else's demands is no longer on your dashboard.

Speaking Your Truth to the Family & Community

During Stage Three you may choose to speak your truth to supportive family members or confront your familial abusers. Depending on the abusive situation, you might choose to speak to your organization or community. It's not necessary to confront the abusers (and in some cases it's not a good idea at all) but it can sometimes be helpful to speak your truth to an abuser in the family or community with others as witnesses, as an opportunity for them to admit what they did and make it right. Listen to your intuition when making this decision to confront or not.

If you decide to take the path of speaking your truth and/or confronting others about the abuse, it's important to expect nothing to change in the relationship or within the other person. You have no control over any of that. Instead this act is about empowering yourself to speak up and face the fear of speaking your truth to an oppressor or to the family and community in which the oppressor lives. If you give this opportunity to the abuser and the abuser refuses to admit what they did and only provides excuses, then you know the abuse will continue if you have any further contact with them because they are justifying their behavior instead of accepting self-responsibility.

Don't expect their validation or even an apology. The abuser is likely not going to own it because if they're a narcissistic character, a lack of self-responsibility is their modus operandus. Keep in mind that your family and community may or may not believe you, but remember that is irrelevant to your truth. If they don't believe you then you know they are not safe for your sanity and wellbeing.

Stand strong in your truth no matter how others react.

Do not not subscribe to their reality if they're trying to minimize it, confuse you, blame you, shame you, guilt-trip you or otherwise pretend it didn't happen. Remind yourself, *that's not my reality!* Then be willing to walk away.

Forgiveness

Working toward forgiveness of self and others is really helpful in this stage. This doesn't mean you reconcile those relationships or keep in contact with the abusers. It also doesn't mean you forget what happened.

No Contact (or in cases where you're coparenting, minimal contact) is ideal. This serves to protect your peace, sanity and wellbeing. Forgiveness has nothing to do with contact or allowing that person in your life. It's about letting go of the heavy feelings like anger, bitterness and resentment that are holding you back from experiencing greater joy and abundance in your life.

When we are still angry and resentful, we are going to keep attracting people who remind us how angry and resentful we are by making us feel angry and resentful. Heavy feelings attract negative karma toward you. It's a dirty, dirty trick that the abuser played by transferring their negative feelings to you through their behavior. Of course you were angry, bitter and resentful because what they did was awful. It's important to recognize that in Stage One, and early on in Stage Two. In Stage Three it's now time to work on releasing any remaining heavy feelings so you can return that karma to its rightful owner and replace the heavy feelings with a new level of peace.

Some people are very adverse to forgiveness and that's okay. Often I hear people express fears of going back to an abuser if they forgive them. That's understandable. Sometimes it's safer not to forgive so you remember why you have to stay away from that person, especially if the relationship is charged with guilt, like a family member. Also, when the abuse has gone on for decades it's possible that you may not want to forgive because you feel too much harm was done.

You might get to the point where you can forgive the abusers you met as an adult because the depth and duration of the abuse was not too long but perhaps you can't forgive your parent because it was too much for too long to ever be made right, especially since they are refusing to change or even admit what they did. Or maybe you were married for twenty or thirty years and so much harm was done in those years that you just don't want to forgive. It's okay. Work to release the heavy feelings left that are holding you back and ruining your days. Remember this is for your benefit, not theirs. The challenge is, can you get it to the point where it doesn't consume you any more and you don't even think about it very often, but when it does come to mind you have the clarity that you were hurt beyond restitution and you don't have to forgive the abuser.

When the fight is over and there is peace of mind, that is what I've come to understand as forgiveness. I'm no longer internalizing the shame of the abuse because I know that's not my burden to carry. At the same time I am very clear with myself that the abusers have no place in my life due to their actions and their inability to change.

Forgiveness is predominantly a gift that you give yourself. The forgiveness comes in layers, just like the healing process. It's not like from today to tomorrow total forgiveness takes place. What's amazing is when you reach the moments when you're spontaneously ready to release negative feelings toward an abuser and those feelings just dissolve or fall away, leaving the space for a new sense of peace, liberation and openness to new possibilities for the present and future. It's important not to forget what happened because that memory is what reminds you that any contact with the abuser/s is dangerous and the same pattern in other people is not to be tolerated.

Self-forgiveness is often the hardest part because we can keep blaming ourselves and regretting our actions but that only holds us in the negative feedback loop. Empower yourself by recognizing that you have now learned from those experiences and you will not react in the same way if something similar were to happen now or in the future. Envision what you would do differently next time, how you would stay in integrity with yourself. This will help you forgive yourself for not protecting yourself and for not showing up in your integrity in those moments. Eventually the self-blame and self-hatred goes away and that's when you know self-forgiveness has taken place.

Self-reliance

By now you're learning much greater self-reliance and you're validating your own truth more than worrying about what others think. You realize what a huge waste of energy it is to worry about what others think, compared to Stage One and even most of Stage Two when you were haunted by thoughts of what others think.

*Your approval barometer is now facing
inward instead of outward.*

Whatever happens now, you trust in your ability to figure it out. You know you have the strengths, tools and awareness to flow with whatever life throws at you and make the decisions you need to in order to take care of yourself and thrive.

Reconnection

Judith Herman wrote, "Recovery is based on the empowerment of the survivor and the creation of new connections. Recovery can take place only within the context of relationships; it cannot occur in isolation."[1]

You are now building a core group of supportive, loving, wonderful people in your Inner Circle and you deeply value those relationships. There is a deep trust between you and those in your Inner Circle. You are creating a new sense of family, even though your tribe may not be related by blood. These people don't play games with you, they don't manipulate you, they don't use you for selfish purposes. They have your back and genuinely want the best for you. They care about you. They don't say things to tear you down or make you small so they can feel better about themselves. Instead they celebrate your successes and encourage you on. They don't depend on you to rescue or fix them. They know they have to do that for themselves.

When you're thriving, your relationships have a win/win quality and they feel uplifting rather than draining.

Stage Three involves a social reintegration as your new self in the community. Nowadays when you meet new people or hang out with your people, you don't talk a lot about the past. You're mostly focused on the present and the future you're creating right now. Now that the past is no longer consuming you, you are able to connect with people who haven't been through narcissistic abuse.

You are now forming a healthy balance of alone time and social time. Of course the balance of this ratio depends on whether you're more of an introvert (you recharge your energy alone and you have a small core group of close friends, preferring to hang out one-on-one or in small groups) or whether you're an extrovert (you recharge your energy around other people and you know a lot of people, enjoying spending more time socially than alone).

Stage Three is also about generating a new spiritual connection with yourself and the universe. By now the devastating sense of loneliness that followed you, maybe all your life, is no longer with you. Every now and then you might catch a glimpse of it but it doesn't last and you know how to shift yourself out quickly.

You're now potentially discovering deep in your mind, body and soul that you are never alone because everything is singing, breathing and dancing together and you are part of it all. You feel a sense of peace and calm even when you are by yourself and even in situations where you find yourself surrounded by people you don't feel connected with. At a deep level you sense your connection to yourself and the universe, as well as the people closest to you in your life and this allows you to thrive like never before.

Unwavering Self-trust

You're no longer easily confused whether people or situations are okay for you. You just know and you trust your inner knowing. It might take you a minute to figure it out in some cases but you will get it quickly then take decisive action to protect and support your peace.

You are no longer willing to sacrifice your peace by second-guessing your intuition when a manipulator is telling you that you're wrong and you should believe them instead. This new level of self-trust allows you to make decisions easily and with clarity.

You no longer let yourself believe what you want to believe because you're now willing to see what's actually in front of you and take action accordingly instead of fantasizing about the potential.

New Relationships

You'll be meeting less abusive and manipulative characters. You'll still run into them occasionally because there are a lot of them out there but you won't let them in as deeply and they won't be saturating your life like before.

Now when you are dating someone new (or inviting anyone new into your life in any capacity) and then suddenly you notice their attempts to manipulate you or disrespect you, you'll have the strength, clarity and self-trust to end it immediately, walking away with your dignity and integrity. You'll be able to leave relationships and situations with gratitude instead of resentments like in the past.

The way people treat you continually gets better
as you consistently treat yourself better.

When people don't meet you with the respect you know you're worth, you'll recognize it immediately and disengage. It won't even sting so much to have to walk away because you'll do it a lot faster before damage was done and you'll feel a lot more confident in your decisions. You won't suffer the aching of nostalgia that you likely felt in the past when you would have to leave an abusive person or situation. In Stage Three it's a lot easier to pick up and move on after disappointments.

Opting Out of Drama

Most importantly, you no longer have the energy to get involved in anyone's games and drama. It's an easy choice to direct your energy and resources toward your passions and purpose, to what feels good and right to your heart because it gives you a sense of meaning.

By this stage you have zero fucks to give about people who are jealous or angry that they're not getting what they want from you or those who are spreading smear campaigns about you because you didn't put up with their abuse.

You're no longer seeking their approval
so it's easy to opt out of their games.

By now you've accepted that you're going to have haters and that's okay because it means you're doing something meaningful. In fact, you laugh at those attempts now. You know how silly they are and you're not falling for it. Your sense of self-trust and purpose is stronger than any hateful comments people make.

You no longer feel the impulse to dim yourself for the comfort of the insecure nor to waste your energy defending yourself from false accusations and provocations. You would much rather opt out of all of that and invest your energy in your sense of purpose and building the life of your dreams while making a difference in the world around you.

Closure

While you'll never get actual closure with the narcissistic abuser because they simply don't let that happen, there are some things you can do to close the circle.

Your closure from the abusive experiences starts by owning your truth even if the other person, community or organization doesn't believe you, refuses to own the responsibility of their actions or even show any remorse.

In the earlier stages you started speaking your truth to professionals and other survivors who understand what happened to you. Now in Stage Three you're more confident to speak your truth to others or even share it in books, blogs and videos.

Don't underestimate the power of speaking your truth. You will see in retrospect just how much the brave gesture of speaking your truth publicly transforms your life and gives others the confidence to tell their stories.

Focus on gratitude to open the path to abundance.

Find something to be grateful for from the experience you went through. You don't necessarily have to be grateful to the person, but the life experience itself. Notice what you discovered about yourself and life and how you transformed your life because of those challenging experiences. Reflect on the powerful lessons learned that you will take forward with you.

When you can create meaning from what happened, you will transmute the trauma into a new sense of purpose. This is where the gold is.

Chapter 16

The Rite of Passage: Stage Three
Reintegration & Return

As you cross the Third Threshold, you return to your Ordinary World but this time as a transformed person with a treasure to share. At the beginning of the Third Stage, you're emerging from the Non-Ordinary World and the deep inner journey where the transformations of Stage Two took place.

By Stage Three, you are no longer living in the same reality as the first and second stages. You were willing to let go of the fear so the shame could die in order to cross the Second Threshold. Then you crossed the Third Threshold where you let go of your attachment to your ego's desires, the old reality and your old self.

Your ego is now giving up more old attachments to your personal limitations and you'll feel a new sense of freedom to live.

Even though you're returning to the Ordinary World where you started this journey, things will never be the same again because you are transformed. The reintegration can be challenging because even though you've changed, life in your community probably hasn't changed much since you began the journey. Now you begin the perilous work of re-entering the community while integrating your new self and new reality, without returning to your old patterns. The tests will come mostly through human interactions.

While Stage One requires some necessary isolation, the catalyst for fully embracing Stage Three is human relationships.

You might even be pursued by vengeful forces, people or things from the past coming back to haunt you as you begin to honor your integrity and protect your peace through action. Your new boundaries and decisions are going to piss off some toxic people, for sure. However, this time the fear of getting in trouble is replaced with clarity, assertion and self-trust.

You now have a whole new level of assertion and the ability to own your reality.

At the beginning of Stage Three, **(11) The Resurrection**[1] takes place. This is where you'll face the last minute danger of falling again. Some sort of magical obstruction usually takes place shortly after you cross the Third Threshold. This will likely take the form of a sudden turn of events or attempts to thwart your progress from the outside. In order to persevere through this test, the most important thing is the stance you take on the inside as you face the chaos on the outside.

The challenge at this test is to maintain **Unwavering Self-trust***.*

In the movies, this is the hero's final and most dangerous encounter with death. Just when you think you're home free, someone or an event tests you one more time.

By this point in the journey you are **Decisive**[2] and you succeed in defeating your enemy, whether it is an internal or external battle, and likely both. As you conquer this test you will emerge from the battle confident, cleansed and steady. You will know that you are a new person and others around you will notice that you've transformed at a deep level.

This is where the Law of Verification will take place again. Have you ever noticed that as soon as you make a shift in your life, when you say goodbye to an old pattern, then it reappears in a different form almost instantaneously? That's the way the universe seems to test us to see if we are committed to the shift or not. It's like reinforcing your position of *I'm done with that.*

There might be more than one event that takes place to test you at this point. I noticed several tests of my decisiveness and self-trust regarding a few relationships in my life, whether intimate, professional or friendships. In these cases my intuition sent me clear signs that something wasn't right and even though I had no proof yet, I listened and acted upon my inner guidance. Within a short period of time, each person revealed to me through their actions that my intuition was right. One of these relationships stood out more than the others.

As soon as I stopped giving the guy in Peru any narcissistic supply in the form of my emotions and instead re-focused my energy entirely on my dreams and projects, he got desperate and tried to emotionally manipulate me and then turn it around on me. It was subtle but I recognized it immediately and told him I didn't have energy for his games. He responded that he didn't have energy to enter into dramas either. I recognized this line as classic blame-shifting and I told him that I was done.

He had a plane ticket to come visit me in a few weeks. The old me would've let him come visit since he already had the ticket and I would've let him in too deeply, minimizing the subtle manipulation signs and giving him the benefit of the doubt until it was too late. This time I decisively put my own wellbeing first instead of worrying about him or taking on the responsibility for the consequences of his actions. I told him this isn't what I wanted, thanked him for the experiences we shared and wished him all the best. He reacted calmly so I didn't block him, thinking that it ended civilly.

The next morning I woke up to numerous missed calls and 25 messages full of nastiness, gaslighting and manipulation. Until that point he hadn't revealed that side of him, but that's probably what my intuition started sensing during my trip the week before.

I continued to maintain my self-control and didn't let him provoke an emotional reaction as he tried to. I didn't respond and I blocked him from any further contact immediately. I could have blocked him as soon as I made the decision to end it at the blame-shifting, but he gave me the hardcore proof. His obvious abuse confirmed my decision and ended up giving me some raw content to share in a video for others to learn from, *Leaving The Narcissist Before The Discard*. Many people commented how helpful it was for them to see those texts in action because it was almost word for word what they'd experienced. I even received private messages from people who thought for sure that it was their ex. That's how similar the patterns of narcissistic abuse are.

It was such a relief to have instant confirmation that I made the right decision to end it when I did, before I actually met that side of him. The low blows and aggression in his final messages were a preview to the plans he had to destroy me over time, slowly and systematically whittling away at my self-esteem, but I took that opportunity away from him so he was pissed. His game didn't work because now I know myself, I trust myself and I believe in myself so I said no friggin' thank you before it ever got to that point. By the time he revealed himself, his words were as insignificant as watching him scream in the rear view mirror as I'm speeding away and leaving him in the dust.

It's so much easier to make the decision to walk away when you trust yourself. Manipulation doesn't work when the self-doubt isn't there. Manipulators are counting on the self-doubt of their targets. They will always test your level of self-confidence like how he tried to flip it around a couple days before when I called out his drama. I owned my reality and didn't back down.

If I had let him visit me instead of ending it when I did, I would have put in jeopardy the energy I invest in my purpose and the contribution I make to others. If I didn't walk away when I did, I would have let him derail me and that would've created unfortunate ripple effects within and around me in my personal and professional life. I also saved my dog from being exposed to another abuser. If I had held onto what my ego thought it wanted (a partner), I wouldn't have chosen what my heart needed (self-love and peace), which at the moment meant being alone again.

For the first time, I walked away with gratitude instead of resentments like in the past. That was a huge growth shift. I believe that was possible because I was willing to walk away immediately instead of doubting myself and sticking around for more.

I am so grateful that he entered my life when he did and encouraged me to go reclaim the places in Peru to clear the trauma from the past. His presence was a catalyst for me to make a massive transformation that I wouldn't have made sitting at home alone. I am grateful that I was able to separate my own transformation from his lack thereof, then recognizing his manipulation attempts and exiting immediately with dignity and integrity so I can keep growing.

It was also the first time I walked away without feeling the pangs of nostalgia and loss that had always plagued me in the past when leaving abusive people, even after dating someone for a few short weeks. This time he wasn't consuming my thoughts, emotions and energy. Instead I felt relieved, confident, free and positive about the future. I felt a revived energy to focus on my passion and purpose and while I didn't know what was coming next, I focused on the essentials and what I needed to do in order to keep moving forward.

Even though he clearly wasn't my life partner because he turned out to be another manipulator, this lesson was totally worth the humbling changes that I was able to make within myself and the new actions I took afterward, opening the path to a whole new life.

By choosing what my heart needed, within one moon cycle, the universe was already filling my life with more of what gives my heart a sense of peace and joy and removing me from situations that were not making me feel alive and energetic.

Within the first couple weeks of ending that connection, I found the strength and courage to divorce my mother, a decision that had been made some time ago but was only waiting my final action. It was groundbreaking. I had several emotionally purging dreams around my relationship with her as well as the dysfunctional family dynamics of abusers and enablers, which confirmed my decision and allowed me to see that my subconscious was finally on board with my conscious mind.

A couple weeks after that groundbreaking action, some surprising events pushed me to move to Mexico City, somewhere I had never imagined myself living. Suddenly I had an entirely different life in a new city, surrounded by new people and a social life. I started feeling a lot more at ease with myself in social situations. My dog has a lot more canine buddies and dog parks to play in. I met an exceptional man who treats me with tenderness and respect as well as my dog. I am so, so grateful I made the decision to walk away from what I thought I wanted because this is so much better than I could have imagined.

At the time that I took action to cut off the manipulator, I had no idea any of this amazingness was coming. Looking back, that was one of the best decisions I've made in my life. By choosing to trust myself and act in alignment with my truth, the universe responded with many blessings.

The Resurrection begins with a decisive action and the results will be more noticeable within a moon cycle or two. Sometimes in the moment it can appear that you lost the external battle by giving something up and not having what you really want yet, but actually you won the internal war with your own demons and that is what changes everything for the better moving forward.

In order to leave an abusive person or situation,
first you have to be able to defeat your internal demons.

Walking away from the abuser or abusive situation is winning but sometimes it's so ugly it doesn't feel like a win. When you're leaving, they will often attempt to make the ending painful and confusing just like that guy did to me.

Abusers try to tell you that you're crazy
and no one will believe you.

They may say this in direct and indirect ways. That serves two purposes for them. One, it might destroy your self-trust enough that you stay or go back to them. Two, it might paralyze you from sharing your truth and telling others what they did to you so their public image remains untarnished.

Manipulators don't want to lose their supply from you so they'll say and do almost anything to keep you there, whether it's idealizing (telling you everything you want to hear) or devaluing (putting you down and making you feel worthless) or alternating between both. Persevere through this storm and validate your perception of reality. Get a reality check from your close friends, the people who actually love and know you. They will help you shrug off those nasty words and remind you who you are so you can keep moving forward.

At this final test, something much bigger
than you is on the line.

You probably sense in a deep place in your soul that if you fail, others will suffer. There may be far-reaching consequences to your kids, your partner, your family, your pets or your community if you choose the old pattern over the new. You'll have to decisively choose between the new strength of character that you've developed or to return and repeat the mistakes of the past.

You have the opportunity to take action and walk away from the old abusive pattern with elegance and grace this time because you know *you got this*. That inner knowing already begins to transform your future, even though you can't see the results in the moment yet.

*Having passed this test, you now know without a doubt
who you are and that nothing is going to thwart
your progress forward.*

After winning the battle, you **(12) Return With The Elixir**[3]. This is the final stage of the transformational process. You've grown so much through your trials and tribulations and you've learned a lot during this journey. You've even faced your own demons and death, physically and symbolically.

You're now living a new life with new possibilities.

You're feeling whole and **Complete**[4] as you integrate the lessons and insights from the journey into your daily life while finding creative ways to share it with the world around you.

The elixir you return with is the wisdom and insights that you've gained in the process and the fresh hope that you're bringing to those who were waiting for your return. This was exactly what was in jeopardy during The Resurrection.

*If you hadn't passed the test of self-trust, you would've sacrificed
The Gift that you could've brought
back to share with others.*

If you're having a hard time making the decision and taking the action to get through that test, think about the people who need you to figure it out. Maybe it's your kids, your partner, your family, your colleagues, your friends or your future following of millions of people online. If you figuring this out can help just one more person, isn't it worth it?

In resolving your own internal issues and defeating your demons, you can now present a new perspective for others to see. The new perspective is key to shifting your reality and giving others a light to find their own way.

The elixir represents your successful transformation and contains the proof of your journey as well as the contagion of faith for others who desperately need it.

The journey would've been meaningless without this nectar to extract, because without integrating your new insights, you would be doomed to repeat the old patterns and you would have nothing to contribute to the world around you.

Several days after ending it with the manipulator it was time to meet my brother on a beach in the Mayan Riviera for the vacation we had planned months before. It couldn't have been better timing. We hadn't been able to see each other in two and a half years since our Peruvian adventure and we were stoked for our time together with nothing to do but relax and hang out.

It's funny how my brother has often shown up in person with uncanny timing right after my disappointments with manipulative guys. It's happened several times now but this was the first time I resolved it on my own and instead of needing back up I just wanted to celebrate.

At the airport on the way there, I saw the manipulator's name on an airplane, another airplane with the name of the city where he was born, and then the first towel guy at the hotel on the beach was wearing a name tag with the same first and second names. I went into the warm, refreshing turquoise salt water and washed him away from my soul.

By the second day of our vacation, I remembered the importance of taking time for relaxation and rewarding ourselves for the accomplishments along the way. We can get easily caught up in the day-to-day stressors, focusing on the negative and what we could've done better, both in life in general and especially after traumatic experiences. That state of tension causes us to become blocked from receiving new information. It also kills motivation and self-confidence. In order to receive new information and opportunities we need to shift into states of relaxation. Rewarding ourselves for the successes along the journey is important to keep building confidence and momentum forward.

The last night there, my brother and I had the amazing opportunity to see baby sea turtles hatching and making their way into the sea. I held one in my hand and could feel its fierce innate drive to survive as it flapped its flippers fiercely.

When they're so small they run the danger of facing predators on land as they make their way into the water and then in the ocean until they grow larger. The care and love that the hotel security staff put into protecting the babies from the predators was touching. Those grown men were as excited about the process as the little kids participating. My brother and I greatly enjoyed the surprise opportunity to witness the liberation of the turtles as they set off on their journey of life. It seemed so symbolic of the journey that I'd just completed and the start of the next one.

The sea turtle is sacred in many shamanic island cultures like Hawaii. They're known for their incredible navigation skills. They're born on a beach somewhere in the world and then travel with the ocean currents for years. They return to the beach where they were born when they're ready to lay eggs. The sea turtle is a symbol of always finding the way home no matter where the flow of life takes you. The sea turtle totem is known to bring good luck and longevity because so few of them survive the predators and perils of the journey. The sea turtle also carries the message that patience with the process is important.

The journey of self-healing, like the journey of life, is a process that unfolds over time, layer by layer. Our human minds may want to rush the process but that will only create more tension. Connecting with nature and observing how animals flow with this journey is a reminder that everything is in divine timing.

Sooner or later, people eventually reveal themselves, even the most covert of predators. It's just a matter of time.

Trust fiercely in yourself and your internal guidance.
You will find your way home to where you belong
no matter how far in the opposite direction you've traveled.
Everything is going to be alright.
Never give up.

At this point in the journey, you may feel like you are fulfilling your destiny moment to moment as you learn to integrate your lessons into everyday life. Remember that you're not done here. You're working on the mastery of these lessons as you move forward. There will be more cycles of transformation to unfold.

You're now looking back at the struggles along the way and you're honoring them as part of your process. You are feeling a deep sense of gratitude to yourself, to others and to life.

You'll be more willing to take risks because you'll understand that if you risk nothing, you learn nothing. You feel confident to take more risks now because you trust yourself. If you're blocking yourself off from the world, you're fooling yourself that you've mastered the lesson. Each interaction with others is an opportunity to put into practice what you've learned and to master those skills better every time.

Take risks through connection with others in order
to grow to the next level.

Your courage in taking new risks will be rewarded with new results. Before you know it, you'll be living at a whole new level that you never imagined possible for you. It will feel like the abuse of the past happened like a distant dream of a faraway land.

Maybe not immediately, but at some point you'll likely receive little messages here and there showing you that the manipulators and abusers were found out and ostracized by someone else, or those who initially doubted you finally realized what you were trying to show them, or perhaps even there is some sort of justice in your favor for what happened.

Sometimes karma is instantaneous and other times it takes time but it always comes back around, I trust in that. If you're lucky the universe will let you know somehow. Just be sure you aren't attached to the idea of revenge or holding on wanting to see their karma returned, because that only keeps you stuck in the negative emotions and the trauma bond. Trust that it will happen in divine timing and keep working on you, focusing on a life of thriving.

After all, the best revenge is living well, continually improving yourself and enjoying your life.

Conclusion

It's interesting how it all comes full circle.

In Stage One of the self-healing journey, there is a necessary strengthening of the ego and sense of self. It's imperative during the first stage of healing to recognize that the problem is the manipulative person with the disorder and not you, reminding yourself that the abuse wasn't your fault. It's necessary to put a label on the manipulator and make ego judgments about who they are in order to gain clarity and dissolve the cognitive dissonance. It's important to strengthen your boundaries and say NO more often to protect your peace.

It's helpful and often necessary to isolate for a period of time during the restructuring of the ego and redefining of the self, the intense research on the topic of narcissistic abuse, as well as the making sense of what happened and the deep self-care work that takes place in Stages One and Two.

By Stage Three you've released your ego attachments to the fears, wounds and and experiences so you can move beyond those patterns. You're reintegrating with others socially and putting into practice what you've learned along the way. Your boundaries are now healthy and clear. You now know you're worthy. Your self-trust is solid and you no longer ignore your inner guidance. Your choices are in integrity with yourself. You're living at new levels of purpose.

The three stages of the journey are like three different realities. When you're in Stage Two or Three, you can forget how you felt in Stage One, which is great for you. However, remember to have empathy for others who are still in Stage One as they're not going to "just get over it" or "just let it go" because they are not ready yet.

Recovery is a natural process revealing itself, much like the journey of life.

The journey of growth and personal development is never really over until we die. When one cycle ends, another begins. We learn and transform one pattern, then we move onto another. Layer by layer we cleanse ourselves and grow. We often revisit earlier patterns and work on them at another level down the road.

There are the macro (Big Picture) transformations and then there are the micro (smaller scale) transformations taking place. In some areas of your life you might feel more like the victim and in other areas you're in the survivor stage, while in another area of your life you may be in the thriver stage. The nature of the healing journey is abstract. As you observe your own transformations, I encourage you to look upon them as if you were looking at abstract art rather than figurative art.

You might notice that you go through the Rite of Passage for every life transformation that you make. Maybe first you go through a spiritual awakening process, then you go through a career transformation, and then you go through the self-healing after narcissistic abuse transformation or in any other order. Perhaps you live to old age and one day you're facing the end of your own life, so you go through a transformational process of acceptance around that.

Through relationships we grow the most. All of your unconscious stuff comes up in the mirror of another person and so you work through more transformational cycles. Maybe you work your way through the self-healing after narcissistic abuse from your ex and/or original abuser, and then you find a new and wonderful life partner so you enter a new cycle of transformation. Then maybe one day you have a child and suddenly new memories and feelings come up from your childhood so you enter another transformation. Maybe you enter a new cycle of transformation due to the death of someone dear to you.

Protect your Inner Circle of people like
your life depends on it.

Don't hang out with people who don't support your success and wellbeing or those who don't want to grow because they will tempt you to stop growing yourself.

There's always the next level that you can grow toward.

If you want to keep growing, continually check in to see where you currently are and aim toward the next level. Remember that the nature of life is change. Everything is in a constant state of change. Don't get complacent in your growth or you will lose your inspiration and ambition. When that happens the universe will often challenge you to spark your sense of passion and purpose again.

Jackson MacKenzie, author of *Psychopath Free*[1] (which is a must-read in Stage One), says the recovery takes about one to two years. Looking at my own journey and the hundreds of people I've worked with personally in coaching sessions, one to two years sounds about right. Don't beat yourself up or give up if you feel like you're not getting there fast enough. Keep working at it consistently and you will see steady progress.

Everything in your life shifts when you have a healthy relationship with yourself. The journey is both internal and external so as you shift the way you relate to yourself, that changes how you interact in the world and how the world responds to you.

The massive shifts out of the trauma take place during spontaneous breakthrough moments. The work you do on your self-healing with structure and consistent, dedicated practice is your preparation for when the one of these sacred moments presents itself to you.

Psychology addresses the dangers of magical thinking. In the case of the rescue fantasy that most victims have, it's true that the magical thinking can be dangerous because it takes away the tenet of self-responsibility and the ability to take action to change your own life. However, as a person who feels deeply connected to the universe, I have also seen how magical moments of life can be. I can't deny the powerful impact of synchronicity, those seeming coincidences when everything aligns to reveal the connectedness of all things the amazing shifts that can result from the right connection at the right time.

For some people, life is randomness and that might be true, but that doesn't make those synchronistic moments any less magical. It's precisely in those spontaneous moments of connection when the biggest breakthroughs from the trauma are possible. This is because the trauma is not managed by the intellectual, logical understanding parts of the brain. We have to go beyond that level of awareness to shift the trauma in massive ways. All the work of consistency and dedication that you do leading up to those moments is your preparation for the opportunity.

It's the fear that's the most toxic part
of the aftermath of abuse.

The fear is the chronic sickness caused by abuse. In psychology they say it's the shame and loneliness at the core and those definitely exist too, but at the very epicenter affecting everything else and holding together the house of cards, is the fear. The fear cannot be resolved at the intellectual level either.

In shamanism, fear and disconnection are seen as the common ailments that humans suffer. Everything negative and toxic originates from there. The fear after childhood abuse is often wrapped up in the absence of a healthy emotional attachment to the primary caregiver/s. The fear of separation from the source of love and nurturing (caused by the rejection, cruelty, abandonment or neglect of a parent or caregiver) leads to the toxic shame and pathological loneliness that a child carries over a lifetime until maybe one day s/he discovers keywords like "narcissistic abuse" after an adult relationship and starts to wake up.

The fear is how we end up hurting ourselves even after we cut off contact with manipulative, abusive people. We try to run from our fears. We wrap ourselves in a blanket of false security to protect ourselves from those fears and in the process we don't allow ourselves to live freely. Eventually the false security falls apart and we get hurt again. Because of our fears, we end up getting in our own way and holding ourselves back. When the fear dissolves in a spontaneous breakthrough moment, the shame dies too.

Until I crossed the Second Threshold, my ego was so attached to those fears holding my reality paradigm in place with the false sense of security that I had built around myself to stay safe from the toxicity of others... but in the moment of breakthrough I discovered that the cosmic joke was *the fear was already inside the gates.*

If you grew up with a narcissistic parent, you were disconnected from a source of love and nourishment and instead you absorbed a lot of fear. Fear was used as the currency of power in the household. Fear is used for control in adult abusive relationships. Fear is also the tool used by the powers that be in the world to keep the human race enslaved and reacting as they want us to.

When your baseline feeling is fear, that's reflected in your self-talk, which creates your perspective. Your fearful perspective then creates your negative reality paradigm. That then attracts a negative vibrational resonance in the world around you so "bad" things, feelings and thoughts keep repeating ad nauseam.

I literally felt nauseated that night in the Andes Mountains when the *wachuma* medicine amplified my awareness of the feeling of the fear and terror that I had been living in all my life. I couldn't stand it any more. So I let it go. It was time.

You can break the cycle.
You and only you have the power to do so for yourself.
It is never too late to start.

We are in this life to learn and grow. No one is perfect. No one is without problems or entirely healed. Anyone who tells you they are done growing and they have nothing more to heal is probably not someone to trust. At best they're not self-aware of their problems. At worst, they're unwilling to admit that they need to change some things about themselves and they're purposely deceiving you into worshipping them like a guru.

You are your own guru. You are the hero/heroine of your story. You are the writer and protagonist of your story. You also need to be able to ask for help when you need it. You need allies, teachers, and helpers who give you faith and nudge you back to yourself through their living example and your interactions with them. Yet you've still got to do the hard work yourself. You've got to rescue yourself.

This journey of self-healing after narcissistic abuse is about creating an entirely new relationship with yourself. It isn't easy but it's totally worth it.

You got this!

THE JOURNEY

Quick Guide to the 3 Stages & 12 Phases

STAGE ONE

1. Ordinary World > Incomplete > Living in Denial
2. Call to Adventure > Unsettled > The Disruptive Truth
3. The Refusal of the Call > Resistant > Caged by Self-doubt
4. Meeting a Mentor > Encouraged > Reigniting Your Soul Pilot Light
5. Crossing the First Threshold > Committed > Self-empowerment

STAGE TWO

6. Tests, Allies & Enemies > Disoriented > Weathering the Storm
7. The Approach to the Innermost Cave > Inauthentic > Meeting Your False Self
8. (Second Threshold) The Ordeal > Confronted > Facing Your Fear
9. The Reward > Reborn > Self-acceptance
10. (Third Threshold) The Road Back > Desperate > The Dilemma

STAGE THREE

11. The Resurrection > Decisive > Unwavering Self-trust
12. Return with the Elixir > Complete > The Gift

Quick Guide to the Three Thresholds

The First Threshold

- This moment comes right after the bottom of the bottom.
- You take the reigns of your destiny back in your hands.
- You own 100% self-responsibility for yourself and your choices.
- You realize that you're not a helpless and powerless victim of life anymore.
- This is the start of self-empowerment.
- As your perspective shifts into a state of empowerment, your reality shifts.
- The hopelessness and helplessness start fading.
- You believe in your ability to figure this out.

The Second Threshold

- This is the turning point in your character transformation.
- It is the moment when you get to the bottom of what has been holding you back.
- You face your biggest fear and that which has the greatest power over your life.
- You drop the blanket of false security.
- Your authenticity cuts through the denial.
- The trauma bond breaks.
- An enormous amount of fear is released.
- The shame dies.
- Your false sense of self dies and a new you is reborn.
- There is an immense relief of anxiety.
- You burn some bridges in order to keep yourself from going back to what hurts you.

The Third Threshold

- This opportunity gives you something new to fight for.
- You face a dilemma and question your ego's attachments.
- What you thought you wanted conflicts with what you really need.
- You are forced to see a person or situation without the goggles of the trauma bond and the underlying fear clouding the radar.
- The Law of Verification invites you to confirm your integrity and self-trust.
- The decision you make is to protect your peace.
- You release the old reality and open to a new reality of possibilities.
- The tension caused by your attachment to your ego desires that was previously draining your energy is released.
- Your self-trust is restored.
- You now own your reality.
- You know that you got this!

181

Como Las Flores
by Shimshai

This is a medicine song about the transformative nature of life that I heard the night in the Andes Mountains when I broke through my understanding about the three stages of self-healing after narcissistic abuse. I wanted to share the message with you.

Así es la verdad, no hay nada que hacer
sino seguir viviendo de la esencia de tu ser
Cuando llegas al final, al final de que no sé
allá te encontrarás al principio otra vez

Así es la vida que viene y se va, como las flores creciendo
nos lleva para donde debemos estar, como el río fluyendo
con cada regalo me encuentro lleno de agradecimiento
y rezo que siga siempre siendo así

Cuando miras al centro de tu ser, dime lo que puedes ver
soltando de lo que fuiste ayer, déjalo ser
Con la corriente de río, todos somos una gota del mar
todos somos una gota de la gran existencia fluyendo hacia el mar

That's the truth, there's nothing to do
but keep living from the essence of your being
When you arrive at the end, at the end of what I don't know
That's where you're find yourself at the beginning again

That's life, it comes and goes, like the flowers growing
it takes us to where we must be, like the river flowing
with each gift I find myself full of gratitude
and I pray that it keeps being like this

When you look at the center of your being, tell me what you can
see
letting go of what you were yesterday, let it be
With the current of the river, we are all a drop of the sea
we are all a drop of the great existence flowing toward the sea

Resources

Intro

1. MacKenzie, Jackson. *Psychopath Free: Recovering From Emotionally Abusive Relationships With Narcissists, Sociopaths & Other Toxic People*, Berkley. 2015.

2. Tudor, HG, https://narcsite.com/

3. Vaknin, Sam, samvak.tripod.com

4. Simon, Dr. George, *In Sheep's Clothing: Understanding & Dealing With Manipulative People*, Parkhurst Brothers Publishers Inc. 2010.

5. Stout, Dr. Martha, *The Sociopath Next Door*, Harmony 2006.

6. Saaed, Kim, *How To Do No Contact Like A Boss: The Essential Guide to Detaching from Pathological Love & Reclaiming Your Life*. 2015.

7. Brown, Sandra L., *Women Who Love Psychopaths: Inside The Relationships Of Inevitable Harm With Psychopaths, Sociopaths & Narcissists*, Mask Publishing. 2010.

8. MacKenzie, Jackson. *Psychopath Free: Recovering From Emotionally Abusive Relationships With Narcissists, Sociopaths & Other Toxic People*, Berkley. 2015.

9. Carnes, Dr. Patrick. *The Betrayal Bond: Breaking Free Of Exploitative Relationships*, HCI. 1997.

10. Jameson, Celia Jameson, Celia (2010). "The Short Step From Love to Hypnosis: A Reconsideration of the Stockholm Syndrome". *Journal for Cultural Research*. 14.4: 337–355 – via Elsevior.

11. Carver, Dr. Joseph, "Love and Stockholm Syndrome: The Mystery of Loving an Abuser", http://drjoecarver.makeswebsites.com/clients/49355/File/love_and_stockholm_syndrome.html

12. Campbell, Joseph, *The Hero With A Thousand Faces (The Collected Works Of Joseph Campbell)*, New World Library, Third Edition. 2008.

13. Office of Resources for International & Area Studies "Monolyth Home" History through Literature Project, University of California, Berkeley. 2010.

14. Vogler, Christopher, *The Writer's Journey: Mythic Structure For Writers*, Michael Wiese Productions. 2007.

Part One

Chapter 3: The Work Of Stage One

1. DeBecker, Gavin. *The Gift of Fear: And Other Survival Signals That Protect Us From Violence*. Dell. 1998.

2. Saaed, Kim, *How To Do No Contact Like A Boss: The Essential Guide to Detaching from Pathological Love & Reclaiming Your Life*. 2015.

3. Herman, Judith. *Trauma & Recovery: The Aftermath Of Violence From Domestic Abuse To Political Terror*. Basic Books. 1997.

4. Campbell, Joseph, *The Hero With A Thousand Faces (The Collected Works Of Joseph Campbell)*, New World Library. 2008.

Chapter 4: The Rite Of Passage: Stage One

1. Vogler, Christopher "A Practical Guide To Joseph Campbell's *The Hero With A Thousand Faces*", memo written to Disney. 1985.

2. Vogler, Christopher, *The Writer's Journey: Mythic Structure For Writers*, Michael Wiese Productions. 2007.

3. Vogler, Christopher "A Practical Guide To Joseph Campbell's *The Hero With A Thousand Faces*", memo written to Disney. 1985.

4. Vogler, Christopher, *The Writer's Journey: Mythic Structure For Writers*, Michael Wiese Productions. 2007.

5. Nolan, Christopher, Emma Thomas, Leonardo DiCaprio. *Inception*. 2010.

6. Vogler, Christopher "A Practical Guide To Joseph Campbell's *The Hero With A Thousand Faces*", memo written to Disney. 1985.

7. Vogler, Christopher, *The Writer's Journey: Mythic Structure For Writers*, Michael Wiese Productions. 2007.

8. Vogler, Christopher "A Practical Guide To Joseph Campbell's *The Hero With A Thousand Faces*", memo written to Disney. 1985.

9. Vogler, Christopher, *The Writer's Journey: Mythic Structure For Writers*, Michael Wiese Productions. 2007.

Chapter 5: Crossing The First Threshold

1. Vogler, Christopher "A Practical Guide To Joseph Campbell's *The Hero With A Thousand Faces*", memo written to Disney. 1985.

2. Vogler, Christopher, *The Writer's Journey: Mythic Structure For Writers*, Michael Wiese Productions. 2007.

Part Two

Chapter 8: The Work Of Stage Two

1. Bradshaw, John. *Homecoming: Reclaiming & Healing Your Inner Child*. Bantam. 1992.

2. Maté, Dr. Gabor. *When The Body Says No: Understanding The Stress-Disease Connection*. Wiley. 2011.

3. Graziosi, Dean. *Growth Summit*. http://growth.com/

4. Burchard, Brendon. https://brendon.com/

5. Witecki, Christopher. https://www.siriusjoy.tv/

6. DiRossi, Portia. *Unbearable Lightness: A Story Of Loss & Gain*. Atria Books. 2011.

Chapter 9: The Rite Of Passage: Stage Two

1. Vogler, Christopher "A Practical Guide To Joseph Campbell's *The Hero With A Thousand Faces*", memo written to Disney. 1985.

2. Vogler, Christopher, *The Writer's Journey: Mythic Structure For Writers*, Michael Wiese Productions. 2007.

3. Campbell, Joseph, *The Hero With A Thousand Faces (The Collected Works Of Joseph Campbell)*, New World Library, Third Edition. 2008.

4. Vogler, Christopher "A Practical Guide To Joseph Campbell's *The Hero With A Thousand Faces*", memo written to Disney. 1985.

5. Vogler, Christopher, *The Writer's Journey: Mythic Structure For Writers*, Michael Wiese Productions. 2007.

Chapter 10: Crossing The Second Threshold

1. Vogler, Christopher "A Practical Guide To Joseph Campbell's *The Hero With A Thousand Faces*", memo written to Disney. 1985.

2. Vogler, Christopher, *The Writer's Journey: Mythic Structure For Writers*, Michael Wiese Productions. 2007.

Chapter 11: After The Second Threshold

1. Vogler, Christopher "A Practical Guide To Joseph Campbell's *The Hero With A Thousand Faces*", memo written to Disney. 1985.

2. Vogler, Christopher, *The Writer's Journey: Mythic Structure For Writers*, Michael Wiese Productions. 2007.

Chapter 12: Crossing The Third Threshold

1. Vogler, Christopher "A Practical Guide To Joseph Campbell's *The Hero With A Thousand Faces*", memo written to Disney. 1985.

2. Vogler, Christopher, *The Writer's Journey: Mythic Structure For Writers*, Michael Wiese Productions. 2007.

3. Cortazar, Julio *La Autopista Del Sur Y Otros Cuentos*. Penguin Books. 1996.

Part Three

Chapter 13: Summary

1. Herman, Judith. *Trauma & Recovery: The Aftermath Of Violence From Domestic Abuse To Political Terror*. Basic Books. 1997.

Chapter 15

1. Herman, Judith. *Trauma & Recovery: The Aftermath Of Violence From Domestic Abuse To Political Terror*. Basic Books. 1997.

Chapter 16: The Rite Of Passage: Stage Three

1. Vogler, Christopher "A Practical Guide To Joseph Campbell's *The Hero With A Thousand Faces*", memo written to Disney. 1985.

2. Vogler, Christopher, *The Writer's Journey: Mythic Structure For Writers*, Michael Wiese Productions. 2007.

3. Vogler, Christopher "A Practical Guide To Joseph Campbell's *The Hero With A Thousand Faces*", memo written to Disney. 1985.

4. Vogler, Christopher, *The Writer's Journey: Mythic Structure For Writers*, Michael Wiese Productions. 2007.

Conclusion

1. MacKenzie, Jackson. *Psychopath Free: Recovering From Emotionally Abusive Relationships With Narcissists, Sociopaths & Other Toxic People*, Berkley. 2015.

Como Las Flores by Shimshai

www.shimshai.com

Made in the USA
Middletown, DE
12 January 2021